You'll find yourself
ling, brutally hone.
uplifting inner and . . . . on the walk of the Camino de
Santiago in Spain.
Jennifer writes with a subtle (almost tongue in cheek) style as she
shares her quest to release her struggling with her own personal
demons. This is sprinkled and spiced with choice spot-on quotes
from numerous spiritual masters; quotes which can inspire us all.
We can identify with Jennifer's inner emotional, psychological
and spiritual gymnastics during her 35-day grueling search for
self-acceptance and self-love. We can empathize and find our
own answers as we walk with her.

—Priscilla Slagle M.D., Private Practice of Psychiatry,
Nutritional and Functional Medicine,
Inactive Honorary Assistant Clinical Professor at the
Neuropsychiatric Institute, UCLA.

Jennifer describes her profound spiritual search on the Camino
with grace and vivid detail—I felt as if I were walking it myself.
And her story inspired me to explore my own existential ques-
tions at this time in my life. I highly recommend this book for its
rich spiritual boost, as well as an experience of the mental and
physical challenges presented by a Camino pilgrimage.

—Carolyn Conger, PhD
Teacher, author, *Through the Dark Forest*

In this gripping spiritual memoir, Jennifer shows us how to let
go, to surrender, and most importantly, to love and accept our-
selves. This book is so much more than a walk on the Camino.
It is a brutally honest and vivid account of a powerful outward
journey and an equally powerful inward one—where the end
is only the beginning.

—Debra Poneman, bestselling author and founder
Yes to Success Seminars, Inc.

This is such a beautiful book. Jennifer Johnson is authentic, bold and inspiring. I found myself feeling that I was with her on this journey—facing my own fear, self-doubt and insecurities—and they were melting away with every day, with every step she took. I love the prayers and spiritual insights. As I read it, all I could think is "When we are connected, we are capable of accomplishing so much more than we think we are."

—Lisa Natoli, teacher, author, *Gorgeous for God*

Anyone who has ever contemplated walking the Camino de Santiago should read this book.
Anyone who has ever questioned "why" should read this book
Anyone who has ever doubted should read this book.
Anyone who has dabbled in A Course in Miracles *should read this book.*
In summation, everyone should read this delightful quest to becoming the true person we all are, which is LOVE.

—Meredith Shay

What a moving memoir of a spiritual journey walking the Camino de Santiago. Jennifer Johnson shares her struggles and her search for lasting happiness with beautiful honesty and vulnerability. I found myself crying and laughing along with her and cheering her on to keep on walking.

—Marci Shimoff, #1 *New York Times* bestselling author of *Chicken Soup of the Woman's Soul* and *Happy for No Reason*

www.winnjourneys.com

AN
AWAKENING
WALK

500 Miles to Self-Love and Acceptance on the Camino De Santiago

JENNIFER WINN JOHNSON

LUMINARE PRESS

WWW.LUMINAREPRESS.COM

An Awakening Walk
© 2018 Jennifer Winn Johnson

Printed in the United States of America

Cover Design: Claire Flint Last
Editor: Jessica Bryan, www.oregoneditor.com

Luminare Press
438 Charnelton St., Suite 101
Eugene, OR 97401
www.luminarepress.com

LCCN: 2017963061
ISBN: 978-1-944733-56-8

I dedicate this book to every woman
who has struggled with self-image.

May we all be at peace.

I am filled with gratitude to
All of my friends and family who supported me
along the way and encouraged me to
"keep walking."

Rachel Resnick and "writers on fire"
for your coaching and getting me to the first draft.

My editor Jessica Bryan,
I knew you were the one for me
the first time we spoke.

All of the towns and people along the way
that support The Camino de Santiago.

My fellow pilgrims

The great teachers and authors
who are quoted in this book.

Table of Contents

PROLOGUE

"It is because you are heavy," Raphael says, so matter-of-factly in his heavily accented English. It stops me in my tracks. I am confused and think I must have misunderstood. No one, a stranger, much less a fellow pilgrim, would ever say such a thing to someone they had just met.

We are walking on a wide, open, grassy path in the countryside. Crossing a short bridge, I am mesmerized by the rushing water, which is loud and powerful and surrounded by yellow and red wildflowers and huge purple hydrangeas.

Raphael is walking with me to practice his English. He is sixty years old, recently retired, and has a wife back home. He has always wanted to walk the Camino. We walk a few miles, alternating between words and silence. The path is quite lovely, very tranquil and quiet, lined with giant trees that provide much-appreciated shade. There are no other pilgrims in sight. We come to a hill and stop to rest for a few minutes to catch our breath. The decline is steep and rocky, which is not my favorite. I take it slowly and carefully – my walking sticks my constant companions.

"This downhill is harder and hurts my feet," I say.

"It is because you are heavy," says Raphael.

I'm confused. *Did he just call me heavy?* No, maybe he meant the way I was walking was somehow heavy, and his meaning has been lost in translation.

Raphael suggests I take my shoes off and rest. "You are heavy and you need to reduce so your feet will not hurt so much." This time there is no mistaking it. He's calling me heavy and I am shocked and dumbfounded.

He knows he has hurt me and proceeds to tell me how much weight *he* has lost since starting the Camino.

"So why haven't you lost weight," he says.

At this point, I want to punch him in the face and scream, "You have no right to say anything about anybody's body unless you are asked for your opinion." After this, I just want to walk alone, isolate myself, which is my habit, and process what just happened

He speaks first, "If I said something to hurt you, I am very sorry. I have disturbed your Camino and understand if you would like to walk alone."

I don't know why, but I stay with him. Perhaps this experience will prove to be a valuable healing, a deep letting go of long-held illusions and emotions.

We are quiet. As we walk, I channel my pain into the simple movement of my body, making it up steep hills strong and fast, as if to say, "Look! Look at what this heavy body can do!"

We continue on, chatting a bit, but mostly we are quiet, listening to nature, the birds, the rustle of leaves, and a far off cowbell. The clouds and shade are gone now and the path turns to asphalt under blazing sun, which hurts my feet even more. It seems to go on forever – how much farther will we walk? There is nothing in sight, except more road.

Jennifer Winn Johnson

PREFACE
The Camino de Santiago

"The pilgrim route is a very good thing, but it is narrow. For the road that leads us to life is narrow; on the other hand, the road that leads to death is broad and spacious. The pilgrim route is for those who are good: it is the lack of vices, the thwarting of the body, the increase of virtues, pardon for sins, sorrow for the penitent, the road of the righteous, love of the saints, faith in the resurrection, and the reward of the blessed.... It rewards those who live simply and do good works."

—Codex Calixtinus[1]

THE CAMINO DE SANTIAGO, ALSO KNOWN AS THE "WAY OF St. James," is the route, or way, taken by pilgrims to the shrine of the Apostle St. James the Greater, located in the Cathedral of Santiago de Compostela in Galicia in northwestern Spain.

---

1 The Codex Calixtinus (written approx. 1138 –1145 A.D. and attributed to Pope Callixtus II.) is an anthology of background details and advice for pilgrims following the Way of Saint James. It includes sermons, reports of miracles, and liturgical texts associated with the Apostle Saint James, as well as practical information.

For centuries, spiritual seekers have believed the remains of Saint James are buried in this cathedral. Walking the Way of St. James was one of the most important Christian pilgrimages during the Middle Ages. Legend has it that St. James' remains were carried by boat from Jerusalem to northern Spain, where he was buried in what is now the City of Santiago de Compostela.

Many people "walk the Camino" in their search for spiritual growth and knowledge, both individually and in groups. The pilgrimage to Santiago is believed to have existed continuously since the ninth century, with the first written records referring to pilgrims from England in 1092 – 1195.

In March of 2015 I became aware of the Camino de Santiago and its potential for my own spiritual development. However, as I contemplated making the pilgrimage, I had many fears and doubts. I also had many questions – and I prayed for answers.

Dear Angels, Guides, and God,

Can I actually do something like this? I mean, the Camino route I'm planning to walk is 500 miles long and I don't even like to hike. My legs feel so heavy, like I'm carrying too much weight. But I suppose this is the point – to let go of the heaviness from hanging onto the feelings, judgments, and anger that are lodged in my body. All this "stuff" literally weighs me down. Is the walk worth it, or is it just one more experience I hope will change my life and make me happy? Because I'm starting to believe that it's just not possible to be happy. I've been told, "With God, all things are possible," but is it possible for *me*? Of course it is. I just need to have faith and believe it's possible. Can I let go right here, right now? Amen.

My Affirmations

*I am free of excess weight. I am free from my past. I let go
and accept Your grace and gifts. I am open to receive.*

Dear God, Goddess, Mother, Father,

Please guide me as to how I can heal the itching rash
on my skin. Is my body letting go of something? A
detox? An allergy? I ask again for your help in letting
go of what is no longer needed. I ask to be of service,
and I ask again about the Camino De Santiago. Please
guide me and show me a sign if this is what I am
meant to do. I suppose if the only thing holding me
back is fear, then I *must* do it.
So what am I afraid of?

1. Not being able to handle it physically
2. Getting hurt, not being able to finish, massive
   pain in my body, failure
3. Being away from home for such a long time,
   especially leaving my dogs
4. Expecting miracles from the experience, and not
   getting any
5. Getting lost
6. Dying out there
7. Exposure to the elements with no relief, especially from the rash on my skin, which is intense
   in the sun
8. Not getting anything from the experience and
   returning home empty-handed

This sounds so negative! Please help me let go of my negative thinking and transform my attitudes. And also help me think of myself as perfect, in the sense that I am exactly where I need to be and doing exactly what I am meant to do. Amen.

Dear God, Universe, Love, and Angels,

What's it really all about, this life? To become a creature of comfort? Surely it is not about amassing more stuff, more wealth. My life is already cluttered. I drive myself crazy with the clutter I create. When I was in the ashram, Gurumayi[2] said that a cluttered room is the sign of a cluttered mind. Well, so be it. I would like to change this.

Why am I afraid to walk the Camino with the big pack? Is this necessary? It sounds like a nightmare. You know I don't believe we must struggle to be close to You, to find and feel You. Am I wrong about this? The answer I receive is, "No." I would really like to enjoy the Camino as much as I can. Of course, it will be hard at times; pain and boredom come to mind, but I think it will also be so rewarding.

As I contemplate this long trip alone, I wonder if it would be better to go with friends. The Camino does

2 Gurumayi Chidvilasananda is the current head of the Siddha lineage established by Bhagawan Nityananda, whose primary disciple and successor was Swami Muktananda. He, in turn, became Gurumayi's guru.

seem to be calling me, but here's another question: should I invite others to go with me?

Walking alone in the open air and learning to let go with Your help; seeing the Divine in everyone and everything around me – these are my foremost wishes. Let me be an open vessel for the Divine to flow through. Amen.

Dear Mother, Father, and Universe,

Thank you for a beautiful morning – it's so nice to sit outside. A beautiful sunrise, a picture painted in the sky, a moving changing picture just like life, always changing. Sometimes we like the way it looks and, well, you know the other. I ask again for help with opening my heart to all. Do I sign up for the Camino, or would this mean isolating myself more? Because I feel like it must be done alone, I think it would be very difficult to do with someone by my side. I know You will be with me, and I presume I will meet others along the way, the perfect people for me to meet. Please show me clear signs if I am to do this – or not. Perhaps I should explore India or Africa, instead.

Please guide me towards love of life, love of myself, and love of my body, towards my dharma and destiny. Help me be and do all that I came here for, and let me radically accept everything as it is *now* and stay present. Amen.

Dear Universe,

Thank you for my home, for a good sleep, and for my dogs. I definitely need a crack in my armor. I need to let go and be vulnerable. How about the Camino? I only heard about the Camino a month ago. Now, after reading several books and researching it, it seems to be all I think about. I've been walking more to test my body, but feel like it could be stronger. How will I manage the Compostela walk of thirty-five days? It's a big walk, a big trip. Amen.

Dear God,

My skin is still itching. If everything is a gift and a lesson, this must be meant to teach me something. I can't imagine it will continue. The signs for walking the Camino are pretty definite – my dogs getting into the scallop shells left over from my catering business and finding them scattered all over the floor.[3] Seeing yellow arrows in random places such as TV shows and videos.[4] These are definitely clear signs.

---

3 From Wikipedia: The scallop shell is a metaphor used by those who walk the Camino. The grooves in the shell, which meet at a single point, represent the various routes pilgrims have traveled, eventually arriving at a single destination: the Tomb of Saint James the Greater in Santiago de Compostela. The shell is also a metaphor for the pilgrim – just as the waves of the ocean wash scallop shells up onto the shores of Galicia, God's hand also guides the pilgrims to Santiago.

4 There are yellow arrows indicating the actual route as it goes through villages, open fields, forests, and rivers. Elías Valiña, the Pastor of O Cebreiro, painted these popular symbols as he walked the Camino (1960–1970). He was one of the most important figures in the revival of the modern pilgrimage to Santiago.

Please guide me as to when I should begin my travel. I really think I should arrange for help from the transport company. The walking will be hard enough, but to know my accommodations and luggage will be waiting for me at the end of each day makes everything seem more doable.

Please empty me of all thoughts that are no longer needed. As I step aside, I let Divine Guidance take over. Amen.

"Your task is not to seek for love, but merely to seek and find all of the barriers within yourself that you have built against it. It is not necessary to seek for what is true, but it is necessary to seek for what is false."

—*A Course in Miracles*,
Foundation for Inner Peace

OUR MISSION, OUR PURPOSE, IS TO GET BACK TO OUR NATURAL state of love – to awaken and come home to ourselves. So what is blocking the love? Our natural state is love – and I do believe it is – but we have piled so much garbage and false illusions on top of it that we have lost awareness of who we really are: love incarnate. One of my personal illusions/false beliefs is that I do not deserve to be happy because, somehow, I am not good enough.

What we focus on persists, and I have decided to surrender to love, to my beauty, to my worthiness, to joy and peace, and focus on what I love: my home, my dogs, spirituality, the beauty of nature, and delicious flavors. I will stop saying food is my blessing and my curse. It is a gift to enjoy good food, and being in a body is a huge pleasure. I surrender to my palette, delicious cuisine, the tastes and smells and creativity of being a chef. I surrender to the process of writing my story as a service to help others. I surrender to the Camino.

"You surrender to a lot of things that are not worthy of you. I wish you would surrender to your radiance, your integrity, your beautiful human grace."

—Yogi Bhajan

Dear Mother, Father, God,

I will walk for You in order to find my way back home to You, and in so doing, remember the truth of who I am, my true self, which is love. I have come to the realization that nothing else really matters, nothing else in this world will ever bring me the peace, joy and happiness I search for. I have tried and I am tired. Amen

Jennifer Johnson, 2017
Rancho Mirage, CA

"Give me whatever is necessary for me to awaken. I don't care what it takes"

—Adyashanti

Arriving in Barcelona

*"A journey of a thousand miles
begins with a single step."*

—Lao Tzu

AND SO THE JOURNEY BEGINS. I WILL BE WALKING THE "Camino Frances," which traverses rural Spain. This is the most popular route and the most supported. The Camino Frances is often recommended for first-time walkers.

I AM IN BARCELONA AFTER AN EXHAUSTING TWENTY HOURS of travel. It is beautiful here, but filled with scattered energy. I do not feel grounded. There is so much going on and I'm sensitive to the noise and crowds. Barcelona will be my home for two nights before beginning the Camino.

After checking into the hotel, I take out my yoga mat and do a few stretches, including my favorite restorative yoga posture: legs up the wall. After practicing yoga for many years and having recently completed a 200-hour yoga teacher training, I have come to the realization that my yoga styles of choice are restorative and gentle. I only want to do easeful movement of my body that is enjoyable to me.

After a brief rest, I venture out into the city towards the sea, the cool breeze and bright sun on my skin. After walking for several miles, my stomach growls, leading me to a café across the street from the beach for pizza – a thin crust with burrata (soft cheese with cream) and fresh basil, a mixed green salad, and wine – of course, wine.

My Affirmations

I now easily and effortlessly release all that's stuck and holding me back. I lovingly make space for what is waiting to come. I open my heart and mind to Divine Grace.

WAKING IN BARCELONA, AFTER TOSSING AND TURNING ALL night, I am nervous about the Camino, especially the first day, which is a strenuous hike over the Pyrenees Mountains. I've been walking and hiking back home more than usual in preparation, but this is not saying much. To be honest, I've never really loved hiking. I like to walk, especially when the purpose is to get somewhere. This is why the Camino appeals to me, as well as the spiritual aspect, of course. Each day on the Camino there is a new destination, a different town or village to experience, and other travelers to meet.

"We are all visitors to this time, this place. We are just passing through. Our purpose here is to observe, to learn, to grow, to love…and then we return home."

—Australian Aboriginal Proverb

AFTER WALKING THE CITY YESTERDAY, TODAY I OPT FOR A fat tire bike tour. Having taken one of these tours in Paris previously and really enjoyed it, I look forward to four hours of touring the city. The guides are young, hip, and

Jennifer Winn Johnson

fun, and the experience does not disappoint. I meet Jane, who is also a solo traveler. Jane is a corporate event planner from Minnesota, who travels many months of the year for events. She is in Barcelona scouting locations for a client. We talk about her travels and she confides that she is concerned about her marriage because she is on the road so much. Her husband is not crazy about it, but she loves her work and feels blessed to have such an interesting career.

After the bike tour, we spend the afternoon walking around the town and visiting the Picasso museum. The Museum Picasso is located on a small street in the bank district of Barcelona. It is housed in a stunning restored medieval palace. For me, the building – with its beautiful architecture, hidden rooms, and courtyards – is as interesting as the art inside. After the museum, we continue walking around town and shop for a World Cup soccer T-shirt for Jane's nine-year-old son.

Saying farewell to Jane, I find a charming café near the hotel that opens for dinner at a reasonable time, early for Spain. Thus, I am the only one dining at 7:00 p.m. Drinking local white wine and eating tapas, I contemplate my life. I have always been a seeker, looking for meaning and asking the universal questions: *Who am I? What's it all about? Do we just live, try to be happy and successful, and then we die?* There must be more to human existence and, furthermore, why is it so difficult to be and stay happy?

"Love is what we are born with. Fear is what we learn. The spiritual journey is the unlearning of fear and prejudices and the acceptance of love back in our hearts. Love is the essential reality and our purpose on earth. To be consciously aware of it, to experience love in ourselves and others, is the meaning of life. Meaning does not lie in things. Meaning lies in us."

—Marianne Williamson

AFTER ANOTHER NIGHT OF NOT SO GREAT SLEEP, I AM READY to get out of the city. The four-hour train ride to Pamplona is quiet and calming. Luckily, I am seated alone next to the window. The countryside is lush with greenery, pastures, and small towns. Upon arrival, I hire a cab for the hour and a half ride to St. Jean Pied De Port, the start of my Camino.

Sitting in the front seat with the driver, who is friendly and kind, we try to communicate through broken English and Spanish. When I tell him I am going to walk the Camino, he raises his eyebrows and says, "Alone?"

"Yes," I reply, and try to explain it's for spiritual reasons. He seems to understand and I see there are tears in his eyes. On our way to St. Jean, we drive over and pass by the Camino trails and many pilgrims. He keeps pointing them out, saying he would like to walk the Camino someday, but as far as I can make out, he has been busy raising a family and never has had the time.

I feel very emotional and try to hide my tears, but the feelings in the car are palpable – our hearts are connected and no words are needed.

When we arrive in St. Jean Pied De Port, he retrieves my luggage and hugs me spontaneously and wishes me "Buen

Camino," the standard Camino greeting. I thank him and tell him I hope he can make the journey someday. I suppose you would take it for granted if it was literally in your backyard. Also, it takes approximately 33 days to walk the entire Camino Frances.

St. Jean Pied De Port is a charming French town and the most popular place for starting this particular Camino route. I will only be in France for one day. Tomorrow, the first day of the Camino, I will cross into Spain as I walk over the Pyrenees Mountains.

St. Jean is crowded with tourists and pilgrims, and filled with many cafés and shops supporting them. Walking sticks, shoes, backpacks, water bottles, scallop shells, and more are offered for sale. I purchase my scallop shell and attach it to my daypack, officially identifying myself as a pilgrim. I proceed to walk around the town looking for the start of the Camino. Not finding it on my own, I feel scattered, like I don't know what the hell I'm doing. Actually, I'm not sure about much of anything right now – my insecurities are up in full force.

Finally, I locate the official Camino office on a steep side street. Many pilgrims are gathered there. The line is out the door, which means there will be many starting from here tomorrow. I register my name and receive my Camino passport/credential, which I will get stamped along the way as the proof needed to receive my "Compostela," which is a certificate of completion. The volunteers who work here love the pilgrims and offer much helpful information. Most have walked the Camino themselves and truly want to help.

Back at the hotel, I unpack and repack my daypack again. What should I carry tomorrow? Snacks, water, and first-aid are a given, but what about an extra pair of shoes, socks, rain poncho, essential oils, and extra shirt. In the end,

I decide to take it all and load my pack to the brim. By the time I'm finished it must weigh 30 pounds, or more!

The hotel is simple and clean, and the innkeepers are especially welcoming to the pilgrims who are about to begin their journey the following day. The walls are thin and I can hear every footstep and voice above, on the side, and below me. My noise canceling headphones are a godsend. I can only hope for a good night's sleep.

Day One

WALKING TO RONCESVALLES, 15.6 MILES/25.1 KM

*"Don't try to force anything. Let life be a deep letting go.
See God opening millions of flowers every day
without forcing the buds."*

—Bhagwan Shree Rajneesh

Dear Mother, Father, God, Goddesses, Angels, and Guides, (I'm covering all the bases here!)

Please walk beside me and give me the strength to make this journey, knowing that with each step I am shedding and letting go of what no longer serves me.

THE FIRST DAY IS THE HARDEST – THE PATH IS STEEP, almost sixteen miles over the Pyrenees with only one place to stop, Orrison. Some people stay here at the only Albergue (hostel), but a reservation is necessary. I did not make a reservation.

Starting slowly – I am not a fast walker and there are many people passing me. This first part is very steep and all on the asphalt. I tell myself to take one step at a time, put one foot in front of the other, stop, rest, and start walking again. The scenery is gorgeous as I move higher and higher.

It's a perfect day, sunny with a bit of cloud cover.

Making it to Orrison at 11:00 a.m., I'm glad I decided in advance not to stay here because I feel strong and want to keep going. Stopping only to rest and fuel up with coffee and orange juice, I sit at a table by myself. After a few minutes, Ren, Ashley, and Lucas, a family from Colorado, join me. Ren, the dad, walked the Camino several years before, and he has brought his kids to share the experience. Lucas is fourteen, tall, and lanky; Ashley is twenty, very cute, short and petite. She confides that she is a bit hung over and does not fully understand what she has gotten herself into. I confide that I feel the same!

I move on, knowing there is a long way to go before the day is done. The path seems to go straight up. The scenery is magnificent and the view expansive, with rolling green hills going on for miles. There are many varieties of birds and fauna, sounds of cowbells can be heard somewhere off in the distance, and the occasional stray cow and donkey cross the road. Seeing many charming farmhouses and cottages dotted among the stunning landscape of the Pyrenees, I wonder what it would be like to live here. I breathe it all in, Mother Nature's beauty, grateful to be here and following this path with no worries about the future. In this place, it is easy to just be present.

This reminds me of *Be Here Now* by Ram Dass, the first spiritual book I ever read. Being only sixteen, I did not understand any of it, but it was the cool "in" book, especially among the spiritual stoners. I think about those years – there is much time to think on the Camino. So much searching, and now here I am still searching, walking the Camino at age fifty-three.

I stop often, my legs aching. The family from Colorado is going about the same speed. They pass me, I pass them, we stop, chat, and move on. I have no idea where I am or how much farther it is to today's destination. The path seems to go on forever. There is a German hiking group nearby. They are very loud, all talking at once, and I can barely stand it after being so silent. I fall back and let them move ahead until their voices fade away. I love the silence and the soft sounds of nature. I walk and walk, and come upon the Germans again. They are on a lunch break. I pass them and keep walking, but they soon come up behind me. They are so loud – how can they listen to each other when they're all talking at the same time? I let them pass again until there is silence – my mind clear, a walking meditation.

Soon my legs and feet feel like they are on fire, I don't know if I can make it much farther. An American group comes up behind me and two of the women walk with me for a while. They are surprised I am traveling alone. They are from Atlanta, Georgia, and when I voice my concerns about making it to Roncesvalles, they offer me positive reinforcement. But soon they are gone, walking very fast, and I can't keep up. Finally, I reach the summit and opt for the easier way down. It's a bit longer but not as steep. I've heard that many people get hurt at this point from descending too fast. I finally hobble into Roncesvalles at 5:00 p.m. It's taken me nine hours to cross the Pyrenees!

By now every step is torture. After walking into the small town and finding my hotel, I check in, shower, and lie down to rest. Suddenly wide-awake, ravenous and excited about dinner, I find the dining room. It's bustling with activity, and I ask to be seated in the far end of the room in order to avoid the noisy German group.

My dinner is a typical pilgrim's meal: insalada mista (green salad), roasted chicken with potatoes and a local white wine, which is well deserved and delicious. I actually feel really good; the endorphins must be kicking in. I can't believe I made it sixteen *steep* miles on my first day!

Oh, and all that extra stuff I packed, I didn't use any of it. I must let go of more, lighten up. This is a great metaphor – letting go of both inner and outer "stuff" is exactly what I hope to achieve on my Camino.

Day Two

"The art of life is to stay wide open and be vulnerable, yet at the same time to sit with the mystery and the awe and with the unbearable pain–to just be with it all."

—Ram Dass

I CERTAINLY WAS ON A HIGH LAST NIGHT, BUT AS TIRED AS my body was, sleep came sporadically. My room or rather apartment was huge, with a living room, kitchen, and two bedrooms upstairs. This did not help as I heard many small noises throughout the night.

Downstairs, the breakfast room is crowded and noisy. Yes, the German group is here. I eat quickly, pack up, sign out, and start walking again, assuming the path will be quite crowded with so many people here today. Passing the famous sign that says "Santiago De Compostela 790 Kilometers," there is no one around to take my photo, so I move on.

MY PRAYER, THIS MORNING

Please remove all of the negativities held in my body, my mind, and my soul. I surrender to God's will and strength to be the best I can be in this lifetime. Amen

THE TRAIL STARTS AS A TREE-LINED, SHADY, MISTY, DAMP path. I walk for a few miles and, incredibly, do not see any other pilgrims. It is actually a bit eerie that it's so quiet. Even though I am alone, I feel like I am *not* alone and something or someone is watching me. At the end of the path, there is a plaque that identifies the area as "Oakwood of the Witches." Evidently, secret covens were held in these dense woodlands during the sixteenth century. It is reported that the wise women healers of the area were burned at the stake in the small town square just beyond where I'm standing for practicing "witchcraft."

The weather is perfect and the walking is definitely easier than yesterday but still challenging. There are many groups and couples walking together, and I wonder what it would be like to walk the entire Camino with a partner. There are many stories of people who have found love on the Camino, and also many stories of break-ups on the Camino. This path certainly has a way of bringing up what needs to come up. Maybe I will fall in love on the Camino. Having never been married or in a long-term, committed relationship, I wonder if this might be my destiny. It really has never been a huge desire for me, but don't we all want to be in love? If it happens, great, but the whole point is to fall in love with my life and myself. Love does not need to come from somewhere outside of myself.

Five hours later, I arrive in Zubiri, having walked 13-1/2 miles. Once again, it's shower, legs up the wall, and foot massage on myself. My feet are sore but doing well. Heading out to get something to drink, I meet the Atlanta group from yesterday and Ren, Ashley, and Lucas from Colorado. I hardly ever drink beer, but somehow it tastes delicious and it is certainly well earned.

At dinner in the hotel, I see Tina from the U.K. We met

earlier on the trail; she is around my age and also walking the Camino solo. She is sitting at a table with three couples from Ireland who are in their fifties and sixties. They invite me to join them and I accept, although I must admit, if I were sitting alone I would have judged them as being too loud. Talking and laughing with them, I feel like I belong – and I look on each one as perfect, beautiful and with love.

Day Three

*"One of the greatest gifts you can give yourself is to forgive.
Forgive everybody."*

—Maya Angelou

Dear God,

Once again, please walk beside me, carry me and show me the truth about myself. Amen

I HAVE BEEN DOING THE WORKBOOK LESSONS FROM *A Course in Miracles* (ACIM) while walking the Camino. Today it's Lesson 101: "God's will for me is perfect happiness." I just have to get my will aligned with God's and I'll be all set!

I recently started studying ACIM again. In the mid-80s, living in San Francisco, I was introduced to the course while attending a New Age church. Along with ACIM, my eyes and mind were opened to many new things in San Francisco. At age twenty-seven, it was exciting to be living in such a beautiful liberal city filled with amazing sights, diverse neighborhoods, foods, restaurants, chefs, and so much more to explore.

My first job was waitressing in a French bistro in the theater district. As one of the few women working there, I was thrilled to be surrounded by so many nice, fun, good-looking guys. I was a bit naïve, at first, and soon found out they were all gay. I had literally never been around the gay culture, never really thought about it. This was 1989 – 1990, and the AIDS epidemic was in full force. The city was filled with fear and heartbreak over the deaths of so many beautiful young men. Within a year of my working at Claudette's, I witnessed the death of more than half of our staff. I will never forget my friend Paul, who was in his early twenties and gorgeous. When he found out he was HIV-positive, he told me with fear in his eyes that the doctor told him he only had a few months to live. Of course, he believed the doctor and passed away a few months later, filled with the guilt of his lifestyle and thinking he did something to deserve his fate. Rest in peace, Paul.

Many authors, teachers, and speakers were writing and teaching New Age principles and the power of love to heal and transform. I could not get enough of all things spiritual: angels, crystals, channeling, past life regression, near death experience, the law of attraction, energy medicine, creating our own reality, and more. At this time, I also discovered several authors, all of whom are still some of my favorites: Louise Hay, Marianne Williamson, Brian Weiss, Paulo Coelho, and Shirley MacLaine.

I also could not get enough of the food scene in San Francisco – the celebrity chefs, the artisan food products, the many restaurants to explore and not to mention the wine country only an hour away. I knew I wanted to be a chef, and I had been to culinary school, but I was intimidated and lacked confidence. Also, I did not want to give up the money I was making as a server for a low-paying kitchen job. So I dreamed and visualized.

It was difficult sleeping last night in Zubiri, only about five hours. What's up with this? I must accept and believe everything is perfect, and trust my body to get what it needs – and also avoid what it doesn't need!

Today at breakfast, I meet a group of Americans and am invited to walk with them, specifically Carey, a woman my age from San Diego. Today's route looks pretty flat, so I put on my Teva sandals to give my feet a break from the boots. The way is beautiful, once again on narrow paths lining the river and wide-open fields filled with wildflowers. The weather is warm and heating up as the day goes on. Carey and I chat about life, interspersed with quiet reflection, during which I repeat my lesson for today, "God's will for me is perfect happiness."

We arrive in Pamplona, the city in Spain made famous by Ernest Hemingway, who wrote in *The Sun Also Rises* about the Running of the Bulls (the Feast of San Fermin), held every July in Pamplona. During this legendary festival, daredevil runners join with the bulls to run through the city streets. It seems a dangerous activity! Pamplona also has many Gothic-style churches, including the fortress-like San Nicolas. This city dates to 75-74 B.C.

It is blazing hot. After leaving Carey, I become frustrated and exhausted from trying to find my hotel. After asking many locals (everyone seems willing to help), it still takes another forty-five minutes to find the hotel and check in. The boutique hotel is gorgeous and I'm thrilled it has great air-conditioning. There is a large bathtub in my room, which I immediately fill with warm water spiked with eucalyptus oil. I doze off while enjoying this luxurious soak.

The evening concludes with another lovely dinner, outside on the plaza, with the same group as last night, and then it's off to bed.

Day Four

WALKING TO PUENTE LA REINA, 14.8 MILES/23.8 KM

"One of the most radical things women can do is to love their body. The truth of the matter is, every moment we spend worrying about our bodies, and not necessarily taking care of them, somebody is figuring out how to take money away from the poor, destroy the environment, drill, frack, burn, rape and violate women, and we are not paying attention. Be radical: Love your body!"

—Eve Ensler

EVEN AFTER A NIGHT OF DECENT SLEEP, I AM EXHAUSTED in the morning and don't want to get out of bed! Knowing a café con leche (coffee with milk) awaits me is my only motivation.

My ACIM lesson for today is: "I share God's will for happiness for me." It reads:

"You do not want to suffer. You may think it buys you something and may still believe a little that it buys you what you want. Today we try to lose its weakened hold still further, and realize that pain is purposeless, without a cause, and with no power to accomplish anything. It cannot purchase

anything at all. It offers nothing and does not exist. Be you
free today to join the happy will of God."

So...why am I walking this difficult, sometimes painful path? Why must I experience so much physical strain? I know the purpose is not to endure pain and suffering for some sort of reward. I'm doing the Camino to let go of pain and suffering, knowing that I have bestowed pain and suffering on myself – the pain of judging and criticizing myself and holding onto false beliefs and ideas about myself. I want to let go of excess body weight, which I know is a symbol of pain and protection. It has served its purpose. Now it is time to let it go, be free, light, happy, peaceful, and joyful. This is truly God's will for us all.

My Affirmation

I share God's will for happiness for me and accept it as my
function now.

It is another hot day as I walk out of Pamplona, knowing I have a very steep ascent up to Alto del Perdon. It is difficult, but it feels really good to be pushing myself, very empowering. I make it to the summit, which is also known as "The Peak of Forgiveness." In this place, iron statues of pilgrims on foot and horseback with their heads bent braving the wind welcome us. A plaque here reads: "Where the weight of the wind crosses the way of the stars."

Today the wind is light, the day is clear, and the views from the peak are stunning.

As I take a few photos and start carefully down the slippery, rocky path, I meet up with Carey and her family and we walk together. The small towns we pass through are charming and quite pristine. I love the façades on the houses and buildings in the small Spanish towns. The façades are made of natural materials, mostly brick and stucco. The personal touches include brightly painted doors and trim, interesting knockers and doorbells, and balconies filled with gorgeous fresh flower boxes. Many homes honor the Camino with tiles featuring scallop shells and yellow arrows pointing the way. I can only imagine what is behind the doors to these homes.

We walk through several quiet towns at siesta time. Where are all the people? They really do completely shut down midday to take a rest.

Leaving Carey, I meet Ren, Ashley, and Lucas from Colorado at Puente la Reina, and we decide to have dinner together in a restaurant in the basement of the hotel. The restaurant is cozy and inviting, with heavy rustic wooden tables surrounded by wine barrels and bottles housed in floor to ceiling iron racks. We dine on classic Spanish tapas: ham croquettes, brava potatoes, and garlic shrimp, followed by traditional paella loaded with seafood and chicken, paired perfectly with a local red wine. Dessert is wonderful: a light orange sorbet and shortbread cookies.

Day Five

Walking to Estella, 13.6 miles/21.9 km

*"Happiness is your nature. It is not wrong to desire it.
What is wrong is seeking it outside when it is inside."*

—Sri Ramana Maharishi

After sleeping well until 2:30 a.m., I'm up at 5:00, packed and ready to go as soon as it is light. Choosing to miss coffee this morning until the first town, which is only about 3 miles in, I'm stocked with snacks, water, and Emergen-C. My daypack is getting lighter every day. Once again, the scenery is absolutely beautiful, and an early start is the best way to beat the heat. The walk is difficult, with quite a few steep hills, but the vibrant green rolling hills, farmlands, massive fields of red poppies, and vineyards are stunning.

Arriving in Estella at 2:30 p.m. hot and sweaty, I check into the hotel and figure a nap is in order. The room is cool and dark. First I turn on the shower, strip off my clothes, throw them in the tub with a squirt of soap, get in and shower – while stomping on my clothes to scrub them. This is my new clothes washing ritual.

Crawling into the comfy bed, I'm wide-awake. It just

amazes me that after walking so much in the heat I cannot sleep. I am told that as a "HSP," a highly sensitive person, it can be hard to get settled in new places. This is especially true in hotel rooms, because there's always a lot of energy floating around in them. Now I completely understand; after being in a different room every night, it makes sense.

Opening my Kindle, I choose one of the many books I have going on: *Letting Go, The Pathway of Surrender* by David R. Hawkins. This seems like a good choice because my intention is to let go and surrender while walking.

"Letting go involves being aware of a feeling, letting it come up, staying with that, and letting it run its course without wanting to make a difference or do anything about it. It means simply to let the feeling be there and to focus on letting out the energy behind it. It is resistance that keeps the feeling going."

—David R. Hawkins

SO MANY OLD EMOTIONS COME UP AS I WALK – FEELINGS of not belonging, thinking I must isolate myself, feelings of unworthiness, sadness, and feelings of not deserving to be happy and joyful. Then there are the many criticisms, shame and guilt: I eat too much, I drink too much, I'm not active enough, I have no discipline, I'm too heavy, and I'm not attractive enough. I feel angry because I have done so much "work" on myself, and this crap is still here, embedded in me. I *know* it is not the truth. It is the ego voice, the small self that holds me back. I know I am strong and have persevered, but, unfortunately, I believed the media and society when they said: *You are only attractive and lovable if you look and act a certain way.* Now I know my dharma, my path, my destiny is to stand up and refuse these lies and help other women and girls refuse them, too. It is a sad epidemic.

I must watch these thoughts as they come up and not push them away, but rather notice them, surrender them, move through them, and let them be transformed.

A Course in Miracles says. "The most sacred spot on earth is where an ancient hatred becomes a present love." This is my prayer and my wish: let me have no hatred or even mild dislike for myself. I am learning to love and accept myself exactly as I am.

Dinner, I'm told, is not until 8:00 p.m. – typical in Spain, but just too late for me. It is 5:30 and I'm hungry, so I head down to the bar hoping for food. The Irish group is there and they invite me to join them. They are so kind and fun, and treat me to several glasses of wine. We drink and share stories, laughter, and tapas. I'm definitely a bit buzzed by the time I'm back in the room. I post some photos on Facebook and add a comment because I thought the waiter in the bar had been rude to me: "I am loving Spain, but the Spanish men can be very chauvinistic towards independent women."

Drifting off, I sleep for nine hours, finally!

Day Six

Walking to Los Arcos, 13.4 miles/ 21.5 km

"The mantra is the master key that unlocks the mystery of the inner kingdom, revealing the fullness of your own heart."
—Gurumayi Chidvilasananda

Waking up after a great sleep, my legs are so tired and sore that I decide to skip the first part of the walk, which is a straight, steep, uphill climb. I take a cab to the top of the hill and walk the rest of the way, which is still 9 miles. Some people might say I'm cheating by not walking the entire way, but I don't care. Let the judgers' judge, and believe me there are plenty of them. This is *my* Camino, and I am listening to my body and taking care of myself.

Once again the scenery is stunning: miles of rolling hills, wheat fields, poppy fields, pristine white and yellow butterflies, and perfect weather – sunny with a light, fresh breeze. Remembering my Facebook post about Spanish men, I feel guilty. After all, it's just my own projection – and just another forgiveness lesson/opportunity. I pray, I forgive, I let it go, and I am rewarded with a divine experience of oneness and acceptance. I look around and realize every-thing is perfect, right here, right now in this moment: every flower, every stalk of wheat, each step, every person. There is beauty all around me, peace all around me; everything is connected in perfect unity. I am humbled and filled with gratitude.

As I continue to walk, always trying to clear my mind, I repeat the mantra of the Siddha Yoga lineage: "Om Namah Shivaya," the Sanskrit mantra that translates as "I honor the Divine within me," and also these affirmations: *I am beautiful and worthy. I am loved.*

MY NEW AGE STUDIES IN SAN FRANCISCO LED ME TO AN Indian guru named Gurumayi and Siddha Yoga. One day, I borrowed a car and drove to the ashram in Oakland. Walking through the door, I immediately had the feeling of "I am home." With the scent of incense, the soft chanting coming in over the speakers in the lobby, and the welcoming staff, I knew it was where I belonged – and that this would be the next step on my spiritual path. I asked for a tour of the ashram and a very nice-looking man about my age offered to show me around.

At the first sight of this guy, Jonathan, I heard a voice inside my head say, "This is the man you are going to marry." I didn't think much of it, but I did not forget, either. He proceeded with the tour, and over the next few weeks we became friends. He was always charming and willing to sit with me and answer all my questions.

Of course, I developed a huge crush on him. At one point, I said something about my feelings and that it felt like he was giving me mixed messages. I asked him about this, and he said he was not interested in me *that* way, but he appreciated our friendship. This was very embarrassing and caused me to pull away from him. Jonathan told me at one point that he was heartbroken because now there was so much awkwardness between us. As for me, I just wanted to avoid him.

I threw myself into the teachings and practices wholeheartedly. I absolutely loved it. I went to the ashram as much as possible, offering "seva" (selfless service), chopping and cooking in the kitchen, meditating, and going to chants and programs. Gurumayi is a dynamic, beautiful, well-spoken Indian woman. Her followers believe she is an enlightened master. She has thousands of followers from all walks of life and from all over the world. She spends most of her time in SYDA ashrams in India and upstate New York.

At the time, she was on tour and would soon be in the Bay Area. She always drew huge crowds to theaters and auditoriums; the lines were out the door to chant with her and listen as she gave a spiritual talk. The culmination of these evenings was "darshan," a Sanskrit word meaning, "keeping the company of the truth; being in the presence of a holy being." After standing in a very long line, often for hours, you would come face-to-face with her and receive her darshan. You could ask a question or simply pay your respects and receive her blessing. Typically, you would bow down and she would tap you on the head with her wand of peacock feathers.

The first time I went up in darshan, I was very nervous, not knowing what to expect. Bowing down, my thought was: *Just bop me and let's get this over with*. Immediately, she tapped me. I stood up, briefly made eye contact with her and walked away. One of her attendees called me back and said, "Did you have a question for Gurumayi?"

Gurumayi was watching me at the same time as she was giving darshan to others in the crowd. I responded, "Well sure, probably like one million questions, but I don't really know what to say."

"Okay," said one her attendees, as I turned and went back to my seat.

This same scenario happened the following two nights. They kept calling me back and asking if I had a question, while I stood there with a deer in the headlights look on my face, my mind empty. Finally, someone said Gurumayi wanted me to talk to one of the staff people. After much cajoling, I realized I wanted to be on staff for the summer at the upstate New York ashram where Gurumayi would be in residence. I lived in San Francisco at the time, but was ready for a change. As much as I loved San Francisco, the crowded city was getting to me after three years and I didn't know what to do next. Summer at the ashram would help me figure out my future.

I ARRIVE IN LOS ARCOS EARLY, 11:30 A.M., AND LO AND behold, a lovely Spanish man shows me to my hotel. Another nice Spanish man at the front desk welcomes me and books me a massage. Thank you for shattering my beliefs and opening my mind and heart. I post this on Facebook, "Sorry about bashing Spanish men. Thank you, universe, for busting my ego!"

Los Arcos is another lovely, tranquil, charming town, with friendly accommodating locals. Sitting in the square for lunch – writing, watching the arriving pilgrims, eating veggie pizza, and drinking wine – it feels like absolute perfection. After a soothing massage and early dinner, it's off to bed.

Day Seven

WALKING TO LOGRONO, 17.3 MILES/27.8 KM

*"The body is a sacred garment. It is your first and last garment.
It is what you enter life in, and what you depart with, and it
should be treated with honor."*

—Martha Graham

AFTER A RESTFUL SLEEP, MY DAY STARTS AT 6:15 A.M.
Today's path is up-and-down, with some rather steep climbs,
rolling hills, and lush farmland. I walk for a bit with two
women: Louise from Canada and Bonnie from Utah. Louise
is petite and fast, and Bonnie is struggling to keep up with
her. I am not as fast and in no hurry, so I let them move
ahead. Running into Bonnie a few days later, she complains
bitterly about the blisters she acquired by pushing herself.
I suggest she take a day or a half a day off and take care of
herself. She refuses this idea; she would rather walk and
complain to anyone who will listen. I, for one, am not willing to listen, so I make an excuse and let her move ahead.

Today the route is almost 18 miles. Knowing this is too
much for me, I decide to stop in Viana and take a cab the
last 4.5 miles. I have decided that about 13 miles is where
my body stays happy, I listen to and honor myself on this.

When I arrive at the hotel, the room is not ready, so I decide to do some exploring. Logrono is one of the larger towns on the Camino, a university town with a population of 155,000. It's also the capital of the famous Rioja wine-growing region. With much to see, I start walking and end up walking right into the Rioja wine museum, which has an attached wine and tapas bar. Thank you Camino!

It's early for lunch and I'm the first customer. The waiter is a charming Spanish man (now it seems they are everywhere!). He asks about my Camino and helps with my order. I decide on a light, fruity rosé and tapas: a seared tuna tataki with a pungent citrus sauce, an interesting variation of the classic gazpacho soup, a baby ham and manchego slider with a garlic aioli, and a roasted red pepper topped with a small piece of fresh grilled fish drizzled with local honey. Typically, ham is not part of my diet, but Spain is very proud of their world-renowned ham, so when in Spain.... There is a flamenco show rehearsing on the stage beside me as I enjoy lunch. The tapas are beautiful, creative, and delicious, the rosé divine. It's such a treat after the typical pilgrim meals.

I eat slowly, enjoying the flavors and the rhythmic dancing of the flamenco show, and after walk around the vibrant city crowded with people on a Saturday afternoon. There is a beautiful square with a gorgeous church, street performers, cafés, locals, and tourists.

I head back to the hotel and get checked in at 2:00 p.m. It's another three-star hotel with good air-conditioning. While checking in, two American men, pilgrims, who did not have a reservation, are basically yelling at the desk clerk and demanding a better room and rate. The clerk remains calm and easily gives them a nice room at the pilgrims' rate. The American apologizes, saying he is hot and tired. I wondered later if he thinks about his obnoxious behavior, which did not represent the pilgrims or Americans very well.

Not wanting to wait until 8:00 p.m. for dinner, I take a nap and go out again around 5:30. Sitting at an outdoor café across from the cathedral – feeling a bit down and lonely, and hoping to run into somebody to hang out with, which does not happen – I grab a light bite and head back to the hotel, stopping in the hotel bar for a glass of wine.

Jay is at the bar drinking a beer; I met him a few days ago and walked a few miles with him. He's a super-friendly, cute guy from North Carolina, probably around forty-five years old. It turns out he is a successful entrepreneur and also a wine connoisseur. He has just gone through his second divorce and is walking the Camino to heal and contemplate his life. He tells me he feels guilty for staying at such a nice place. He has not slept in days because he has been staying at the crowded Albergues, and he has been walking on badly blistered feet. So tonight he has decided to treat himself. He tells me he feels like he is cheating! I tell him, "Then I should feel guilty every night!" We have a good laugh and nice conversation. He is going out to meet people for dinner, so we say goodnight.

Later someone tells me that Jay has become quite the celebrity on the Camino. He is very generous, and he's been treating the younger, broke pilgrims to drinks and dinner almost every night. Many of the people on the Camino are on tight budgets – you can definitely do the Camino fairly cheaply if you choose to. Obviously I chose the more comfortable way.

Day Eight

WALKING TO NAJERA, 18 MILES/ 28.9 KM

"There is a huge amount of freedom that comes to you when you take nothing personally."

—Don Miguel Ruiz

I WAKE UP EARLY AGAIN, KNOWING I WOULD PROBABLY sleep better without drinking wine. But this is one of my issues, one of my addictions: filling up and anesthetizing myself with food and wine. The thing is, I really enjoy good food and wine, and feel good while imbibing. I just overdo it a lot!

MY PRAYER

If I am meant to stop drinking wine, please give me the desire to stop – or help me let go of the guilt around it. I surrender this, Amen

DURING THE SUMMER OF 1993, WHEN I HAD JUST TURNED thirty-one, my application to spend the summer at the Siddha Yoga Ashram in upstate New York was approved quickly and things moved fast. I packed up my flat in San Francisco and flew to New York for the three-month commitment. I was nervous and excited because I knew it would be a mind and heart opening experience. I also assumed it would be healthy, because the food served at the ashram is vegetarian, nourishing, and tasty.

My mother asked me before I left whether there would be wine at the ashram.

"Nope, no alcohol for three months."

She looked at me wide-eyed, knowing that I have a pretty regular wine habit. However, I was actually looking forward to a bit of a detox.

I was assigned to a room with three other women – basically the room had two bunk beds, four small dressers, and one bathroom. On some of the busier weekends, they put two extra mattresses for visitors on the floor in the already crowded room. The ashram was scheduled to be jam-packed with thousands of people coming from all over the world to partake in courses and programs, to offer seva, and, of course, to be in the presence of Gurumayi.

I knew there would be difficult times at the ashram, but as the devotees say, "It is all part of the fire." The spiritual path is not easy. Going to the ashram can be blissful, but sometimes you feel the Guru's fire. At the time, I was shy and intimidated about pursuing my cooking career. "Don't worry," many of the devotees told me. "The Guru will burn it [your doubts] out of you."

The first few weeks, I was given the seva of early morning fruit chopping, which meant I was alone in a small room at 5:00 a.m. cutting fruit and making fruit cups for the crowds. It was actually quite blissful and serene, very quiet and peaceful. It was a beautiful way to begin the day.

After a few weeks of fruit seva, I was assigned to work

in the Amrit (a small café) kitchen. When you are a guest at the ashram, your meals are included and served in a large dining hall. But there is also the Amrit, where you can buy more specialty items. I loved working in the kitchen with many cooks who had been around the ashram for a long time. I learned to cook delicious Indian food and was given free rein to create specials for the café. Frankly, there was no time to be insecure or intimidated, because there was so much work to be done. Later, after I had left the ashram, I realized my insecurities around cooking had definitely been burned out of me.

About two months into the summer, I realized that I was losing weight, although it was really not an issue, because I just felt so happy, accepted, and peaceful. While serving food one day, there stood Jonathon in front of me holding out his food tray – remember, my future husband from Oakland?

The first words out of his mouth were, "Oh my God! You've lost like thirty pounds!" I was taken aback; first of all, because it was probably more like twenty pounds. I was also shocked that this would be the first thing out of his mouth when he saw me again – like anybody has the right to say something like that to another person. It is out and out "fat talk." I realized with dismay that my weight was likely the only thing he had seen about me, and I could not help but think it was why he had not been attracted to me when we first met. I suppose he was looking for a smaller girl. His rude comment was just one more confirmation of my negative beliefs about myself.

After three months at the ashram, I felt incredible, just like I'd hoped. My mind and heart had been opened and my future looked bright. I was lighter in body, mind, and spirit. When my mother picked me up at the airport, the first thing she said was, "Oh my God you are so thin. It's a dream come true." Apparently, this was my mother's great dream for me.

Unfortunately the dream did not last. Being back in "real" world the weight crept back on slowly but surely.

TODAY IS A LOVELY DAY FOR WALKING. I MEET AND WALK with Terry from Florida and Andy from Ireland. We all keep about the same pace and have a pleasant, subdued conversation.

Arriving in another charming city, I see my hotel is quaint and boutique style. The innkeeper, another charming Spanish man, who is very welcoming, walks me to my room carrying my luggage and asks me about my Camino experience. The help and kindness of the people on this trip is heartwarming. Some of us really need to wake up and realize that to have love and kindness in your life, you must be kind and loving. It's really so simple.

Arriving in Najera at lunchtime on Sunday, I sit at a café by the river and watch families, children playing, pilgrims arriving, friends having a beer – animated in their conversations, and young lovers sharing an ice cream and a kiss. The whole scene is quite lovely, safe, and blissful. I sit alone, wondering what life has in store for me, what the Camino has in store for me, and remembering my wish and intention to be present, stay present, every step, every town, each person, see God in all.

MY PRAYER

Dear Universe, show me the truth. The truth is all I seek. I walk for this peace, joy, love, acceptance, and kindness. Amen.

Later I have a lovely dinner at a restaurant around the corner from the hotel, although again I wish dinner was available earlier. The menu this evening starts with garlic soup: a rich broth filled with peppers and onions, very light and comforting, (I must try this recipe at home), followed by a delicious grilled chicken skewer, which is simple and filled with smoky garlicky flavor. Of course, there is wine. The waiter asks if I want red or white, and then puts a whole bottle of red with no label on the table. The wine automatically comes with dinner. In case you have not figured it out yet, there is mucho vino on the Camino.

Day Nine

"Constant kindness can accomplish much. As the sun makes ice melt, kindness causes misunderstanding, mistrust, and hostility to evaporate."

—Albert Schweitzer

AFTER BREAKFAST AT THE HOTEL, I AM OUT THE DOOR AT 8:00 a.m. Only a few other pilgrims are leaving this morning, the temperature is lovely, sunny blue skies with fluffy, snow white clouds. Walking out of town, I notice a local woman about eighty years old leaving the church. She stops and looks at me with the kindest loving smile. "Hola," she says. "Buenos Dias, Buen Camino." She walks beside me for several minutes pointing the way, even though it is clearly marked. Such a sweet, supportive, simple gesture; she wants to help, to be of service to a pilgrim. As I wave goodbye and thank her, the tears come as my heart breaks wide open.

The path today takes me through vineyards, more wheat fields, and fields filled with vibrant red poppies and other wildflowers. The vines are filled with baby grapes, the first stages of a delicious Rioja wine. The way today is quiet. I pass a few pilgrims and several more pass me. At one point,

I hear English behind me and know Americans are coming. They approach and the guy offers me a peach, which I accept. As always, we offer each other the official Camino greeting, "Buen Camino." I ask them, "American?" "Yes," he says. "Where from?" "California." "Me, too, where?" "Palm Springs?" "Oh my God, what? Me, too!"

It's such a small world. This is my first meeting with Heather and Craig. We walk and talk together for a few miles, and when I take a break after a steep uphill they move on.

Making it to town, my feet begin to ache again. As I sit and change into my sandals, Heather and Craig show up and sit with me. They hand me their contact info and say they hope we will see each other again.

When I find my hotel, I see it's not all that great. It's noisy, but clean, and once again the innkeeper is kind. Thinking maybe some shoe inserts would ease the pain in my feet, I spend the afternoon visiting the shoe store and exploring the town.

Making my way to the "plaza mayor" or Main Square, I find the perfect spot for writing: a patio at the Parador de Santo Domingo. A "parador" is a kind of luxury hotel, typically located in a converted historic building such as a monastery or castle.

It is beautiful and majestic, so why am I not staying here? It's a peaceful hour, and the church bells just rang telling me it is 6:00 p.m. The sun is still high and bright, and the square fills with locals just returning from siesta, mothers with strollers and small children, and pilgrims. You can always tell the pilgrims, because they have changed into flip-flops and they are limping along – this is known on the Camino as doing the "pilgrim shuffle."

How lucky and blessed I feel, thank you, thank you, thank you.

THE INNKEEPER HAS ARRANGED AN "EARLY" SEVEN O'CLOCK dinner for me, and she is waiting when I arrive back at the hotel. She leads me downstairs to the empty dining room and brings out local red wine and water, a plate of sliced salami and a large plate of vegetables, green beans, carrots, and sliced potatoes. The vegetables are overcooked but a nice change. It seems that fresh vegetables are not usually on the menus intended for pilgrims.

She also brings bread, of course, bread, which is served at every meal. The next course is a simple salad. Next, she brings chicken, saying in broken English, "This is my specialty, pollo con mi salsa especial." It is absolutely delicious, and when she comes and asks how it is, I say, "Yes, yes, very good, muy bueno." We communicate with words and gestures. I have a translator app on my phone and use it to say, "I feel your heart in your food." I don't know if she understands, but she smiles warmly and seems happy that I am enjoying her creation.

Nobody else comes into the dining room for dinner, and I feel honored and taken care of. I tell the innkeeper, "Good night; muchas gracias."

Back in my room, I post some pictures on Facebook. This has become my nightly ritual, and I am getting a bit of a following and much support and encouragement from back home. I sleep soundly until 5:00 a.m.

Day Ten

Walking to Belardo, 14 miles/22.4 km

"Let silence take you to the core of life…. But Listen to me. For one moment quit being sad. Hear blessings dropping their blossoms around you."

—Jalal al-din Rumi,
The Essential Rumi, New Expanded Edition

Getting started today at 8:00 a.m., after a simple breakfast of coffee, fruit, and toast, I say goodbye and thank the innkeeper/chef. She wishes me "Buen Camino" and hugs me warmly. Outside, it's another beautiful day. After walking a few miles in my boots with the new inserts, my toes are feeling completely squashed and my feet are throbbing. I find a bench and change into my sandals, freeing my feet so they can breathe. About halfway through the day, I stop and eat a power bar and an apple because I don't feel like being around the energy of a bar. Now remember, a "bar" in Spain is also the name for a café.

I continue repeating my mantras and prayers, and putting one foot in front of the other – not going too fast. Once again, I am alone on the trail and cannot see any other pilgrims. It is so silent, just the sounds of a light breeze and singing birds. I am slowing down, getting really tired, and not feeling very motivated. Looking at the map, I see there is still another 7 miles to go. Feeling like I might topple over, I begin wishing for a taxi to come and pick me up, but there is nothing in sight except the path. Just when I think I cannot take another step, out of the blue a woman from Japan comes up behind me and says hello. We walk and talk for a few miles. She helps me so much. She is a Camino Angel.

THE HOTEL IS LOVELY, ALTHOUGH MY ROOM IS ON THE third floor and there's no elevator, which means walking up the stairs with my backpack and luggage is difficult after already walking so many miles! Once inside, I immediately lie down on the bed with my legs up the wall; my feet and legs are throbbing. A hot shower follows, stomping on my dirty clothes, more gentle yoga, and rest.

Self-massage on my feet and skin with Spanish extra-virgin olive oil feels fabulous. My dry skin is thirsty for moisture and the oil soaks right in.

I feel like having a quiet evening in my room because I don't want to eat alone again in a busy restaurant. I head out to buy some food and run into Heather and Craig, who are staying at the same hotel. They invite me to join them for dinner. We have a lovely time talking, telling stories, and laughing. It seems we have some of the same family "issues," but I suppose everyone does. Now that I am here on the Camino, away from my family, I am thinking of them, missing them, and loving them.

Day Eleven

WALKING TO SAN JUAN DE ORTEGA/24.2 KM

"If a single person achieves the highest kind of love, it will be sufficient to neutralize the hate of millions."

—Mahatma Gandhi

WELL, ACTUALLY, I'M NOT WALKING TODAY. I SLEPT REALLY well, eight hours straight through, but it seems to have made me even more tired this morning. Then, at breakfast, the rain started – the forecast is not good for today. A French woman is standing outside the hotel asking for a cab and I opt to join her. This is the perfect opportunity, because a day of rest is much needed.

The cab drops us at a bar/café, which is also the reception area for my next hotel. It's in a very small town that has one bar, one hotel, one Albergue, and one beautiful Cathedral. The bar is super loud and crowded with people trying to get out of the rain. I order a mineral water and add my Emergen-C packet and a few drops of ginger essential oil. I am told my room will not be available until 12:30, which means waiting two hours. I cannot imagine sitting in the bar for so long. It is now pouring down rain, so I run to the cathedral, which is breathtaking, and has been a shelter for pilgrims for hundreds of years.

Sitting in one of the wooden pews, worn smooth from years of worshipers, I light a candle and repeat my *Course in Miracles* lesson for the day, #108: "To give and to receive are one in truth."

"To give and receive are the same." This means that when we offer something to others from our hearts, we will receive the same in return. For example, your prayer might be:

"To everyone, I offer quietness."
"To everyone, I offer peace of mind."
"To everyone, I offer gentleness."

Make your offerings slowly, pausing after each one. They will come back to you in proportion to the degree you offered them."

I continue with these offerings, adding several more that are also dedicated to everyone: love, compassion, warmth, grace, health, abundance, lightness, friendship, and happiness. After an hour, my mind is empty and still. I continue to sit in the cathedral meditating, feeling peaceful and grateful.

BACK IN THE BAR TO PICK UP MY KEY, WHO WALKS IN BUT Jay from North Carolina. He is soaking wet from walking in the rain for hours and does not look happy. He seems incredulous that I am dry – and that I did not walk in the rain! Perhaps I am cheating again.

My room is simple and quiet, with French doors that open onto a balcony overlooking the countryside. I open them and listen to the rain. Transported to another time, I can feel the energy of those who have walked this path before me, and I am humbled. Many emotions well up from inside me – I let myself feel them and cry until I fall asleep.

There is a Spanish proverb that says, "How wonderful it is to do nothing and rest afterwards." I agree.

At dinner, I sit with Isobel, a young woman just out of college and Ashley. Ashley has now split off from her dad and brother, choosing to walk with the young pilgrims she has met and who have formed a strong bond walking the Camino together. We speak about our lives, hopes, and dreams. They are both at a crossroad in their lives and the Camino is helping them make some tough decisions. I treat them to dinner and feel like a "Good Camino Mama."

Day Twelve

WALKING TO BURGOS, 16.2 MILES/26.1 KM

*"There is only one rule on this wild playground...
have fun, my dear, have fun."*

—Hafiz

NINE HOURS OF HEAVENLY SLEEP IS A GIFT. RAIN IS STILL in the forecast, so I'm debating about taking a bus or a taxi. After drinking a café con leche, I decide to walk. I feel fantastic and filled with energy and it looks so nice outside. Taking off alone, there is no one in sight and the heavily wooded trail is especially quiet. After about 2 miles like this, seeing absolutely no one, I feel a bit scared. It amazes me that with all the people walking the Camino you can walk for miles without seeing another person. I pray and surrender my fear – offering peace of mind, joy, and happiness to everyone – and my fear lifts, allowing me to embrace the quiet and absolute stillness all around me.

The weather is cool and brisk, and I am able to keep a good pace until I come to the small town of Atapuerca, which has been declared a UNESCO world heritage site. The earliest human remains ever discovered in Europe were found in the prehistoric caves located here. It is still early, so nothing is open, but there are several pilgrims hanging out. Once again, I have no idea where they were while I was walking. I start up a hill, and it's a pretty good climb on a rocky path.

At the peak of the hill, there is a large cross, a pile of stones, and an altar. I say a quick prayer. The sky gets darker as I begin the descent. Stopping to put on my rain poncho, a light rain begins.

Just as I come to a fork in the road, two Irish women come up behind me. They are looking at the map, and I join them in deciding which way will work best. We decide to go left and walk together as the rain and the wind become ferocious. There is no shelter anywhere and at least 2 more miles to a town. Needless to say, we get soaked and it's freezing. We stop at the first bar we find, where many other pilgrims are also seeking shelter. I order a coffee and inquire about a taxi. Another lady from Canada hears me and says she will share it with me. So for about $8 each, we get a ride into Burgos and are dropped off at our respective hotels – it is money well spent!

Burgos is a fairly large city with a population of 180,000. The most known landmark is its breathtaking French Gothic Cathedral dedicated to the Virgin Mary. I had been told it was a long walk from the outskirts to the center, and the walking is right on the highway and through an industrial area. So I am very happy for the taxi ride.

My room on the third floor is nice and there is a much appreciated elevator. After a hot shower and a little rest, I venture out to find something to eat. Walking around town, I run right into a Thai massage place. Miguel, the masseur, says he will be available in forty-five minutes. Typically, I love Thai massage, equating it to a great yoga practice with someone else doing all the work, but this time it is incredibly painful! I know Miguel was trying to help, but he found points on my legs and feet that I did not know even existed. In the end, all of it was good, and I'm sure he helped my sore, tired feet and legs.

Heather and Craig are booked to stay in Burgos for a few days, and we definitely want to spend the evening together as I am continuing on the next day. And so we do, with much wine, tapas tastings, stories, and laughter, while cruising the many bars of Burgos. We stay out late, until 11:00 p.m. It is hard to keep track of time because it is still light out. They walk me back to my hotel, big hugs are exchanged, and we promise to keep in touch and meet again when we return home. It has been a fun, beautiful night on the Camino with new friends.

"What you do today is important, because you are exchanging a day of your life for it."

—Source unknown

Day Thirteen

"I have learned this, at least by my experiment: if one advances confidently in the direction of his dreams, and endeavors to live the life he has imagined, he will meet with success unexpected in common hours."

—Henry David Thoreau

WAKING UP EARLY, I AM DEFINITELY FEELING THE WINE from last night. I had arranged to meet Anne, blister Bonnie (I make this reference because she is still talking about her blisters), and Lori for breakfast at 7:00 a.m. I had met each of them on the trail a few days before. They also met each other on the trail and agreed to walk to Santiago together. They invited me to join them today. I thank them, accept and explain that I also like walking alone, so please do not take it personally if I decide to split off and go on by myself.

It is a bit confusing when getting out of the bigger cities, and it takes us over an hour just to find the quiet path again. By this time, I have had enough chitchat and am craving the quiet and inner work again. I stay with them until I have had enough talking. I don't mean to sound harsh, but some people have a tendency to tell their stories and talk about their problems over and over again, and remember what you focus on will persist. So, please, let the past go!

They move ahead of me, and I'm back to walking alone and continuing my offerings and my ACIM lesson today # 109 "I rest in God" which I repeat and add, "I rest in peace, I rest in love, I walk for God, I walk for peace, I walk for love."

I send my offerings to everyone on the planet by going through the alphabet. I offer everyone: authenticity, beauty, compassion, delight, ecstasy, fun, greatness, happiness, imagination, joy, kindness, love, magic, niceness, openness, purpose, quietness, renewal, silence, timelessness, understanding, vision, wisdom, excitement, youthfulness, zaniness.

Then I go through the alphabet again, over and over, coming up with every offering I can possibly think of.

I hope this does more for my friends and fellow pilgrims than listening to each other talk about their aches and pains.

I enter the meseta, which is basically nothing but wide-open endless crop fields of wheat and barley, and not much shelter. It's a long stretch, and it takes about five days of walking to get through it. I have heard that many people pass over this part of the Camino, but I am actually looking forward to it. Today I find it quite beautiful and very quiet, only the sounds of birds and a light gentle wind can be heard. It's the perfect place and time to let go, to surrender, to open and receive.

AFTER BEING AT THE ASHRAM FOR THE SUMMER, I DECIDED to move to Santa Fe, New Mexico. Amy, my sister had been living there for a few years and she really loved it. I was excited about the new possibilities, and I immediately found a serving and bartending job on the central plaza at a restaurant that was famous for their margaritas and Mexican food. We rented a classic adobe style house in a great location, adopted two rescue dogs, and the Santa Fe adventure began. With its great restaurants and food scene, world class art galleries, the bluest sky ever, unique architecture, spirituality and yoga, mountains and desert, Native American and Mexican influences, I fell in love with Santa Fe – which is also known as: "The city different." I kept up with my Siddha Yoga practices of meditation and chanting – mostly to CDs while driving; my car became my chanting studio – and visited the ashram a few times a year.

TONIGHT'S HOTEL IS A FEW MILES FROM THE TOWN OF Hornillos. I call the hotel and they pick me up. It turns out the group from this morning is also staying here. We arrange to meet for dinner. The time for talking is over dinner, and a great dinner it is: a tasty potato soup, followed by perfectly seasoned chicken cutlets served with a beautiful organic green salad lightly dressed with a sherry vinaigrette. Lori is a vegetarian and she is having a hard time because the Spaniards, especially in small towns, are not very vegetarian friendly. Here, they make her a beautiful meal of eggs scrambled to perfection with sautéed mushrooms and salad, she is thrilled. We have a local white wine to top it off and a delicious caramel flan for dessert.

Day Fourteen

"To live this life. To live it with wholeness and gratitude and trust. In the pain and the glory. In the mess and the grace. In the sacred and desperation. This is the stuff of which real superheroes are born."

—Jeanette LeBlanc

I WAKE UP AT 4:00 A.M., AFTER MUCH TOSSING AND TURN-ing, feeling anxious for the breakfast hour to come. I am ready to get walking. I would have left early and eaten on the road, but we are off the path by several miles and I did not want to add the extra distance.

The group from last night arrives in the dining room at 7:30, along with a few more pilgrims. We have a good breakfast and the innkeepers drive us to the Camino around 8:00 a.m. and I start out walking with Lori from San Francisco. I really enjoy her company and find we have much in common talking about organic food, living in San Francisco, and walking the Camino. She is around my age, married with seventeen and nineteen-year-old children, and she is in between jobs. It's the perfect time for her to walk the Camino.

We stop about 3 miles in for a photo, and then I am ready to be on my own again. I talk to Lori about this and she completely understands, she is a bit disheartened because she has committed to walking the whole way with Anne and blister Bonnie, and now feels like she would like to be on her own as well.

I DO NOT UNDERSTAND WHY ANYONE WOULD SKIP THE meseta. It's quite lovely, although a bit muddy from the rain. Right now, most of the wheat is a beautiful light green/celadon color, and with the light breeze you can see the stalks waving for miles. It is very beautiful and serene.

Walking at my regular pace, I notice an interesting man passing me. He is walking very fast and looks to be of Asian descent. He's small and has a colorful scarf wrapped around his waist. Perhaps he is a monk, or at least very spiritual. As he walks by, he gives me a huge smile, and says, "Buen Camino."

I think, now that is someone I would like to talk to, but he is walking much too fast for me. I do not think much about it until I come to the first small town with an open bar. I order a coffee and look for a seat outside, and there he is, sitting alone at a table and watching me.

I approach him and say, "Do you mind if I sit with you?"

He makes a welcoming gesture to please sit. He speaks fairly good English and asks where I'm from – while looking deeply into my eyes. His name is Mark and he is from Iran. I ask how long he has been walking/traveling and he tells me twenty-three years! He proceeds to show me his passport, and all the pages that are stamped with places he's been: India, Bhutan, Europe, and Africa. He tells me he has been walking the Camino for a year, and he proceeds to show me all of his pilgrim passports with stamps from Portugal, France, and Spain. He says he is a nomad and travels with only his backpack and a tent. He offers massages and fire ceremonies to make a bit of money. He graciously accepts when I ask if he is hungry and offer to buy him breakfast.

As we sit and drink our coffee, Mark looks at me and says, "I can tell you are searching for something more in this life. Something spiritual."

I nodded my head, "Yes, yes," and we speak about how the walking is a meditation and people talk too much on the Camino! We both agree that the time to talk is when you stop to rest and eat, and at the end of the day. But walking should be silent, listening only to the wind and the birds, letting go of the chatter of the mind, yes, yes, yes! He is quite funny when he mimics the people who talk loudly on the Camino, "blah blah blah blah."

He is staying in this town for the evening, so I bid him farewell and "Buen Camino." He gives me a stunning smile and a warm hug. Maybe our paths will cross again. I believe Mark is quite an inspiration, he lives his life exactly how he wants to. He is happy and completely present.

I WALK ALONE TO CASTROJERIZ, ENJOYING THE SERENENESS all around me, appreciating each moment, every wildflower, every leaf on every tree. I notice each purple, white and yellow butterfly, fluttering their wings effortlessly, each one unique, perfect and peaceful. The butterflies, no thinking, completely present to the air, the flowers, not concerned of the human eyes on them. So lovely, I believe this is spiritual bliss.

The last mile before town involves walking on the road, with occasional cars whizzing past way too fast. It is very disturbing when you are in this peaceful state of mind. I will try and avoid road walking at all costs from now on.

Arriving in town, I'm hungry again – I seem to always be hungry on this Camino. I thought I was going to lose a lot of weight effortlessly, but now I am rethinking this. And I have to say, several of the other women I've met are also hoping to lose weight while walking the Camino. We talk about this as we are eating and drinking wine. This was a big hope for me too, but now I realize it doesn't really matter, because the Camino is giving me so much more.

I find my hotel and the room is clean and well furnished. I rest, shower, read, do some light yoga, and wait until 7:30 for dinner. By this time, I'm feeling extremely tired and hungry, and debating whether I should just go to sleep early. Deciding on dinner, I make my way down to the restaurant and chat with a pleasant Japanese couple. The husband tells me he has been planning to walk the Camino for over ten years, and now here they are, finally. He is very happy and grateful. I am not sure how his wife feels, she is silent.

I eat quickly, another Pilgrim meal of garlic soup, roasted chicken, and French fries. No dessert tonight for me. It's back to my room for a quick Facebook post. If I miss a day, my friends tell me they start worrying about me, so I make sure and post at least a few photos and words every night before I go to bed.

Day Fifteen

WALKING TO FROMISTA, 15.5 MILES/24.9 KM

"Listen, God loves everything you love and a mess of stuff you don't. But more than anything else, God loves admiration. I think it pisses God off if you walk by the color purple in a field somewhere and don't notice it."

—Alice Walker

I'M LEAVING TODAY AT 7:00 A.M. AS IT IS 15.5 MILES, SO AM starting out with no breakfast or coffee. I walk out of town with Lori, chatting a bit at first. As we swiftly move up a strenuous and steep couple of miles, we are completely silent feeding off each other's energy. Arriving at the top, we are rewarded with a beautiful sunrise view back over the valley floor and the town.

We walk on in silence for quite a while, until we come to some picnic tables. A Spanish couple with a young daughter has set up a stand, and they are selling coffee, fruit, and drinks for donations only. I have a cup of coffee and an orange and give them a generous donation. From what I understand, the unemployment rate is high in Spain, and I am happy the locals can make some money by feeding the pilgrims.

We continue walking and are getting close to a small

town. We are hungry for breakfast, and as we enter the town, the owner of a café excitedly points our way to her establishment. We probably would have stopped at the first place on the road if we had not seen her motioning to us. Smart move, her place is warm and welcoming, we order delicious coffee and an American breakfast of fried eggs and potatoes with a tasty garlic sauce. It hits the spot!

As we continue to walk the meseta, I hang back as Lori is chatting with another pilgrim and once again I'm craving silence. Listening only to the silence, I try to empty my mind and be completely present. The sky is a brilliant blue with snow white clouds, and the fields seem to go on forever. As thoughts of past events and people come into my mind, I let them go again and again. I am letting go of what no longer serves me. The old beliefs pop into my head: *Who do I think I am? I am not worthy. I am not pretty or thin enough. I am lazy, on and on...* and I let the thoughts come, so I can look at them and release them. I repeat, "Om shanti, Om shanti, Om mane padme hum." I say my mantra, "Om Namah Shivaya," with each step. I ask for help in letting go and loosening my grip on the old thoughts and beliefs that have held me back. I cry and keep on walking.

An Incident In Santa Fe

I HAD A WAITRESSING JOB AT ONE OF THE BEST RESTAU-rants in town and was making really good money, but I really just wanted to cook. I started putting my name out for catering and picked up a few little jobs here and there. I finally realized that waitressing was just not for me anymore, and that at some point I had to take the leap and quit. At one point, during the middle of a busy shift, I stopped in the middle of the restaurant and said an urgent prayer to God:

I can't do this anymore. It's breaking my spirit in half. It's killing me, and I need to get out of this job. Please help!

Within a few weeks, I had quit the job and started up a catering lunch business to get me through. Soon I was picking up more and more catering jobs and was able to support myself. I realized later that my desperate heartfelt prayer was the catalyst for this change. It was such a great lesson. It felt like God was telling me: *All you have to do is ask for what you want and then hand it over to me.* A *Course in Miracles* says most of us do not ask for too much, but rather we ask for way too little. It's really quite simple. When you have faith, life can be enjoyable and easy.

I CATCH UP TO LORI AND WE STOP FOR A QUICK REST, water, self-foot massage, and a change of shoes. We have 3 miles to go to Fromista in order to make it a 16-mile day. Lori's energy is great. She is walking at a good pace and I am able to keep up with her. Together, we experience the perfect blend of silence and good conversation.

We arrive at 2:45 p.m. and, surprise, we are hungry! We check into the hotel, shower, and meet again for a late lunch. Lori, who is really not drinking on this trip, decides to share a bottle of wine with me, and I wonder: *Am I a bad influence?*

The cold, crisp Verdejo at six euros per bottle is delicious and so inexpensive! We each have a pilgrim meal of mixed green salad and spinach lasagna – this is a new and unique pilgrim meal so we are pretty excited about it! The food and wine are excellent, the company superb, and the afternoon and setting is perfection.

Back in my room and feeling fantastic, I open the windows to a light breeze and a view of the church. I rest and listen to the square filling back up after siesta time. I am content and feel very blessed.

Day Sixteen

Walking to Carrion De Los Condes, 12 miles/19.3 km

"When the time comes that nothing goes forth from you other than that which you would be glad to have return, then you will have reached your heaven."

—Ernest Holmes

After sleeping well, I get up early to read, meditate, and catch up with "Words with Friends." The girls and I had made arrangements to meet for breakfast, but they are late and arrive talking on and on about which route to take. This goes on day after day with them, and frankly I'm tired of it. I have learned on this path that you cannot look too far ahead – you must focus on being in the present. All the talk is jarring to my ears. I excuse myself with, "Buen Camino. I'm sure you'll catch up to me," knowing full well it probably won't happen.

I decide on the alternative path, which is off the main route and looks like it might be quieter. There are only a few pilgrims, and I wish peace of mind and letting go of fear for everyone, and to myself, as I continue walking.

When the path takes me through a ghost town village, I become frightened. It feels quite eerie, like someone is watching me, although there is no one else around. The air is damp and misty as I quickly walk to the other side. I stay on the path, which is quite muddy from the rains. This is "stick to your boots mud," and it slows me down quite a bit because I have to knock the mud off my boots every few steps. I am definitely ready for a coffee, and turn onto a road signaling the way back to the main Camino route. There's no coffee to be found, so I just keep walking, my feet and leg pain returning once again.

The weather is quite foreboding, chilly and cloudy, and it feels like it is about to rain. I come to a small town, Villalcazar de Sirga, as a light rain starts to fall. I order a coffee at the bar and sit outside in the drizzle. I see the French couple who stayed at my hotel a few nights before. They wave and we communicate through eye contact and kind smiles.

I visit the beautiful Knights Templar Church of Santa Maria, sit for a while, and get my passport stamped by the local priest. I have another 3.5 miles to go today. The path is gravel and next to the highway.

My Affirmations

I am love. I am peace.
I am as God created me, eternally free and unlimited.
Peace, love, and joy abide in me. I Am that I Am.

Carrion De Los Condes comes into sight just as the wind and the rain are picking up. I make it into town and realize I have at least another mile to walk, all the way through the town to get to my hotel. I am feeling quite exhausted and walking slowly. Finally making it to the hotel, I discover I have hit the jackpot for tonight! Monasterio San

Zoilo, is an absolutely stunning monastery that has been turned into a hotel. My room is ready and it's delightful. There is a large, inviting canopy bed and massive windows, which open to a view of ancient trees and the sounds of leaves rustling in the wind.

I make my way downstairs for a late lunch at the restaurant and splurge on grilled vegetables with ramesco sauce, a delicious potato chive soup, and a perfectly chilled Verdejo white wine. There are only a few other diners in the restaurant, all single men. I'm not sure if they are pilgrims or businessmen; everyone smiles and says hello, but otherwise it is a quiet lunch. Afterwards, I walk back to my room and enjoy a luxurious bubble bath and a nap.

After resting, I explore the expansive grounds and halls of the hotel. It all feels very familiar. I feel serene, comfortable, and contemplative. I wonder: *Have I been here before?*

I'm feeling a bit run down and decide to sleep in. I might even skip walking tomorrow. The monastery hotel is so beautiful that I ask to stay another night, but they are completely booked. I definitely want to come back here again.

Day Seventeen

WALKING TO CALZADILLA DE LA CUEZA, 12 MILES/19.31
KM

"Understand that the right to choose your own path is a sacred privilege. Use it. Dwell in possibility."

—Oprah Winfrey

AFTER WAKING UP IN THE BEAUTIFUL PALACE THAT IS
Monasterio San Zoilo, I contemplate the 12-mile walk to
Calzadilla, which I know at this point I can easily walk
in about four hours. I could take a cab and rest up in
the next town, but it is a very small town. If I get there
too early and the room is not ready, there will not be
much to do.

The breakfast buffet is just about the best on the
Camino, so I load up and even splurge on a chocolate
croissant.

I decide to walk. Leaving at 8:45 a.m., the way is flat. I
am still in the meseta and supposedly there is a mobile café
about halfway. The path is long and straight and mostly
shade-less. It has warmed up again today and there are no
clouds in sight. Repeating my mantras and affirmations, I
walk.

My Affirmations

Stay present, let go.
I am tired. NO! Change that thought.
I am filled with peace, light, and strength.

Four hours, 12 miles, easy, keep it going, easy. I am in rhythm with my mantra: Om Mane Padme Hum. I am love. I've got this! I love my feet. I love my legs, no blisters! I am so proud of my feet, my strong legs, my hips opening and getting into each step easily and gracefully.

I must be halfway by now. Where is that café? I need to rest, but there is no café in sight. I come to a picnic area with a bit of shade and see Isobel. She is full of smiles and hugs, and introduces me to two new friends. They are just finishing their break and they're off. I rest for fifteen minutes, eat a quinoa granola bar, and walk another few hours to arrive at Calzadilla.

It's a quiet town with not many cars, but a few tractors can be seen working in the fields. I find my hotel, a hostel with a lively bar crowd. There's Isobel, the Japanese couple, the single Japanese man I keep running into, and the German guy, who is much friendlier than he was a few days ago.

I check in and drop my luggage in my clean room with poor lighting – it's nothing like the "palace" was last night. I head down for a cold beer and snack, and sit at a table with two Spanish women from Pamplona. They are biking the Camino for one week. They ask where I am from, and one of the women, Maria, says she has been to Los Angeles and it made her cry. She says there's a huge difference in the way the people there live. Some of them have enormous houses and so much money, but there are also many poor people living on the street. She says that in Spain it is more even, and the people who do have a lot of money do not flaunt it. I agree with her that it's sad. America, the land of big dreams, is certainly a nightmare for many.

The owner and staff at this place are fantastic, fun, and welcoming. The owner has walked the Camino several times and you can tell he loves serving the pilgrims. He exudes kindness and warmth. What a treat! The accommodations are so different from last night, but the service makes up for it.

I head up to my room for a shower and a nap. I'm looking forward to dinner and more interaction with these folks.

SANTA FE, 1997

AFTER THREE YEARS IN SANTA FE, MY SISTER GOT MARRIED and I moved out to a private ranch forty miles outside of town. I had catered a few times for Anne and Mason, the owners of the ranch. They liked my cooking and me, and asked if I would come live on the ranch and be the ranch chef. I jumped at the opportunity. Their ranch is a 6,000-acre working cattle and horse ranch, where they host many private guests, as well as several five-day horsemanship clinics in the summer. When my friends asked if it was a "dude ranch," my response was, "A dude ranch meets Ralph Lauren and the Ritz."

The ranch was stunning, and they set me up in an apartment at the end of "the line house," one of the many homes on the property, which had been built recently. On one end, there was a large recreation room with a pool table, jukebox, games, cushy couches, a gorgeous stone fireplace, and a state of the art dream kitchen. Anne asked me to set up the kitchen and stock it with anything and everything I wanted or needed – money did not seem to be an issue here! I was encouraged to use the kitchen, have fun, experiment, and try new recipes.

There were five hotel-type rooms between my apartment and the kitchen. They were usually empty, but available for guests and friends, when needed. A huge covered porch filled with rocking chairs and an organic garden surrounded my apartment and the kitchen. Basically, I had the whole place to myself. My dogs and I were in heaven!

It was busy in the summer with guests coming and going, which was a lot of work and a lot of fun. I was in my element and getting many compliments on my food flavors and presentations. I cooked everything you can think of: cowboy camp breakfasts, grilled pizza and organic salad lunches, Southwest and Italian buffets, and four-course wine-paired dinners. One more bonus: Mason was a wine connoisseur with a world-class wine cellar and he loved to share! Sometimes, I thought I would stay there forever!

When business slowed down at the ranch, I was alone much of the time. I began to feel like I was enjoying the isolation a little too much, so I decided to move on. Forever had turned into three years.

AT DINNER IN CALDAZILLA, I SEE LESLIE FROM WASHING-ton, a woman I had met briefly earlier in the day, and a redheaded American man named Charlie. We decide to eat together, and when we enter the dining room we see a huge pan of noodle paella filled with mussels and rings of calamari. We take a table, and soon we are each served a plate of food, along with what else: a bottle of the local red. I love this country. It's part of the culture to drink wine with most meals. I don't know why I have some guilt around enjoying wine so much, we are supposed to enjoy life, right?

The dining room is lovely and filled with the great energy of pilgrims having a good time. A few more join our table: an Italian man and Ingrid from Holland, who is now living in Spain. The paella is our starter course. Next, the choices are lentil soup or salad, and then chicken, beef, or fish. To be honest, the food is fairly basic (as most pilgrim meals are), but the energy and love I feel is generous and openhearted, and it will not be forgotten. There are a few birthdays – one is Leslie's, and we sing, clap, high five, and offer "Buen Caminos" all around. I do not deny myself dessert tonight – the ice cream sundae is delicious. We all hug, say goodnight, and are off to bed.

Day Eighteen

"It is hard to recognize that thought and belief can combine into a power surge that can literally move mountains. There are no idle thoughts. All thinking produces form at some level."

—*A Course in Miracles*

After a good six hours of sleep, and then tossing and turning for a while, I'm up at 6:00 a.m. to read, meditate, and study the route for the day. It's amazing how much I can look at the guidebook and then forget everything once I start walking. Once again, I believe this is a big lesson on the Camino: let go of the past and future, stay present, be here now!

Walking through the meseta, I chant, I affirm, and I thank my body. I thank God for this life and this experience. I ask for guidance on the way forward.

My Prayer

Help me stay present and remember that all is good, right now.
Help me know there is no need to worry about the future.
Help me stay present! Thank you

I walk and I hear someone approaching. It's the Japanese man I have been seeing for the past few days. We walk a bit together and finally ask each other's names. His name is "Suzuki," I say, "Oh…like the motorcycle?" He laughs and says, "Yes, yes." He seems like a kind man.

He asks why I am walking the Camino alone. I am not sure how to answer, so I give my standard, "midlife crisis." He nods thoughtfully and we continue on. He tells me he walked the Camino ten years ago and felt like he wanted to walk again before he is too old. He tells me he is seventy-eight!! I would have guessed sixty-five. He tells me he is happy to see many more Japanese people on the Camino this time. We walk together a while longer, until I see a bench and stop for a brief rest. Suzuki moves ahead and along comes Leslie. Like me, she is also walking the Camino alone.

Leslie tells me she is having a hard time because she has put on weight recently and she is walking with a large pack. Leslie feels like she is not in very good shape for this level of commitment to physical activity – and she is also hoping to lose weight. We talk about women and bodies, and how we have bought into the ridiculous standard of beauty that has somehow made us feel "less than," inferior to others. We certainly do not fit the body type idolized by the media and the fashion industry! I offer a prayer on behalf of all women. We are all unique and beautiful, please let us embrace ourselves exactly as we are.

My Prayer

Please God – let me except myself as I am. I have wasted so much time and energy on criticizing myself. Please help me reach my full potential.

Jennifer Winn Johnson

AFTER A FEW MILES WITH LESLIE, I MOVE AHEAD, ENJOYING the peace and beauty all around.

As I stop to change into my sandals, giving myself a break, Ingrid from Holland now living in Spain appears. She is yet another woman walking the Camino solo. We walk together for a while, and I really enjoy her quiet energy. She has walked different routes of the Camino four times. She tells me about the Portuguese route, which she walked for two weeks last year. My mind is already turning toward the future. I love this way of traveling.

The town for tonight is Sahagun. I find my hotel, drop my bag, and head down for lunch. The room is dingy and dark, and there is constant running water from the toilet and buzzing from the light bulbs.

Oh my God! Well…okay. I will have to deal with it, but right now I need food. Eating hurriedly, I have lunch sitting next to two Frenchmen. From what I can understand, they are driving the Camino backwards.

Back in the room, it is even noisier than before. I try putting on my headphones and it's still uncomfortable. I walk downstairs and politely tell the clerk about the toilet. He comes up with a toolbox and tries to fix the plumbing, but it's not getting any quieter. Finally, he hands me a new key and walks me across the hall to a new room – and, literally, I mean a new room. It's completely renovated, clean with large windows, a fabulous bathroom, and air-conditioning. The terrible room has been changed into a lovely one. *Thank you, Camino.* This is a big lesson for me: *I must not be afraid to ask for what I want.* I shower and nap, and decide to stay in tonight. After resting, I'll go out and find a market, purchase some snacks for the evening, and go to bed early.

Day Nineteen

Walking to El Burgo Ranero, 12 miles/19.5 km

"The universe says, Allow me to flow through you unrestricted and you will see the greatest magic you have ever seen."

—Klaus Joehl

I SLEEP WELL AND AM UP EARLY FOR BREAKFAST AT 6:45, which consists of café con leche, fresh OJ, and a chocolate croissant. It's delicious and I thoroughly enjoy it with no guilt.

Today I will be walking only about four hours on flat ground, still in the meseta. I walk alone in silence for two hours, passing only a few pilgrims along the way. Stopping for a quick break at the halfway town, it is warming up again, so I order a refreshing sparkling water and add my Emergen-C packet.

Around the corner comes Ingrid from Holland, now living in Spain. We walk and talk – mostly she talks and I listen as she goes on about her family and how her sister and niece are "bipolar." She keeps saying it with her fingers up in the air making quote marks around the word "bipolar." They live in California in a very affluent city. They are on medication because they're both "bipolar." Ingrid assumes and asks if all people in California are "bipolar." The niece was a lawyer and then she became "bipolar," so she went into a clinic, or "What do they call it?" she asks. "Rehab" I say. "Oh yes, rehab." Now the daughter is renouncing the world to become a nun and marry Jesus. The mother supports this because, as a devout Catholic, she is proud that her daughter is going to be with God.

The daughter chooses a convent on the East Coast that is completely closed off, no visitors allowed, and as far away from her family as possible. It turns out the parents pushed her into a high-powered school and career; they also pushed her brother into becoming a pro golfer, even though he just wanted to go to Paris and be an artist. Now the sister is off to be a nun and the brother is thirty, living at home, depressed, and "bipolar." Apparently, he was never good enough to be a pro golfer and his dreams of being an artist and Paris are long gone. Her father is not happy about this.

This is just a note to parents who think they know what is best for their children!

I agree with Ingrid that there is an epidemic in America. Bipolar mania and depression, rehab, pharmaceutical drugs, and antidepressants are big business.

Several years ago, I was mildly depressed and experiencing a lot of anxiety. I was working with a trainer who recommended a therapist. Thinking it might be a good idea, I made an appointment. The therapist was an older man, and asked why I had come to see him. I spoke for about a minute before he interrupted me, saying, "Would you like me to prescribe you something?" I looked at him dumbfounded and said, "No, I am here because I want to work through this." His response was, "Wow, how refreshing," He offered me some lame exercises. I paid and never went back.

BACK TO WALKING – INGRID AND I WALK TOGETHER UNTIL we find our hotel, but the rooms are not quite ready. We sit outside watching the line form across the street at the Albergue. I have not actually seen how they work. I have heard you can make a reservation at the private ones, but the municipals and public ones (the most inexpensive) are first come, first serve. You simply set your backpack down and form a line. When the owner/manager (hospitalario) opens, he welcomes everyone, lays down the rules, and invites four people at a time to check in.

In the meantime, my room is ready and it's quite comfortable. After showering, I continue to watch the line at the Albergue through my second story window, while slathering my skin with olive oil. I hear it's a daily race to get to the Albergues, because they fill up quickly. This is definitely not my style.

I plan on meeting Ingrid for a late lunch, knowing now that this is a better plan for me – a late lunch and then a light snack later before bed. At lunch, the dining room is filled with locals and pilgrims. Included is a plate of blanched leaks with a few sliced tomatoes, this is the only vegetable on the menu, unless you count the fries that come with the fish. I take an orange to my room for dessert.

I get into bed and put my legs up the wall. My feet are sore, deep down to the bone sore. I am feeling a bit down, just kind of blah, and I'm not sure why. I cry over some silly thing I read, hoping and praying that the deep sadness in me is being released. I never leave my room again that evening, but stay in and eat the leftovers from yesterday: a bit of bread, a can of tuna in olive oil, almonds, and a half bottle of wine. I use the blackout shade and turn the lights out at 9:00 p.m.

I wake up several times during the night remembering my dreams. They are weird, vivid dreams of expanding bugs and spiders that need to be killed immediately or they will multiply and invade us, and also dreams of death and funerals and burials. As I am waking up at 5:00 a.m., I realize these dreams signify something inside of me, something ancient that is being released, dying here on the Camino.

Day Twenty

*"Wine is constant proof that God loves us
and loves to see us happy."*

—Benjamin Franklin

I meet Ingrid for breakfast, grab some fruit for the road, and we walk out of town together. We talk for a while and then separate, although I know she is close behind me.

I drank a lot of water, OJ, and coffee at breakfast, and now I really need to pee. There are no toilet facilities for several miles, so I find a hidden spot and squat. When I come back to the trail, Ingrid is waiting for me.

"OH MY GOD HOW CAN YOU DO THAT?" she says.

"What? Pee?"

"I could never!"

"After all the hiking and walking you've done, you've never had to pee on the trail?"

"No way I would, or could, ever do something like that! How could you?" says Ingrid.

I am completely dumbfounded. After we get over the pee incident, we continue to walk together and she gets on her sister subject again. On and on she goes. She also tells me she is a Buddhist and she is not judgmental. I think she has some judgment here, but then I suppose I am judging her for judging! Really, it's all just one big mirror going round and round in the circle of life.

She starts talking about religion and asks me if I believe in God.

"God is such a stupid concept," she says. "In Buddhism we do not believe in God."

"Do Buddhists believe in not being judgmental?" I say, adding, "Yes I believe in God, but not in a fundamental religious sort of way."

I decide our discussion is complicated and try to leave it at that. The last thing I want is to try and explain my beliefs to Ingrid from Holland, now living in Spain.

MY PRAYER

Please help me let go of judgment, self-righteousness, and criticism. Help me recognize and remember that we are each on our own journey, and that we are in exactly the right place at the right time, and with the right people.

BY THE TIME WE MAKE IT TO THE NEXT TOWN, MY LEGS and feet are sore again. It's another charming village: a twelfth century, medieval, walled city. When we arrive at the hotel – a small family-run bed and breakfast – the host welcomes us with a smile and offers each of us a glass of wine. I accept, Ingrid rolls her eyes and does not.

The innkeeper says my room is ready. Ingrid has also booked a room, but he informs her that she will be staying at another hotel up the street. As I enjoy my wine, she argues relentlessly, and he just smiles and lets her go on, explaining that there is no room for her at this hotel. Finally, she gives in, and he takes her to another hotel. Secretly, I am kind of happy about this.

Before she leaves, we make a date for a late lunch ninety minutes later. The inn is an old house with only four rooms. It's cluttered with antiques and memorabilia, and it's quite charming. My room is on the street side, second story, with a rod iron queen-size canopy bed and deep red brick red walls covered with old pictures and portraits. I lie down immediately with my legs up the wall and do some light stretches on the bed. I bathe in the tiny shower – it's barely big enough to turn around in – and head down for lunch.

In spite of being such a small place, the dining room is spacious and holds about fifteen tables. It is popular today, filled with many locals. I can see why – the food is delicious: a fresh chunky gazpacho, warm whole grain bread, a mixed green salad with a light vinaigrette, and fresh grilled fish with a tasty herb sauce served with perfectly ripe sliced tomatoes. The food is simple and fresh, this is "farm to table" at its finest. After telling me on the trail that she does not drink often because it's too fattening, Ingrid has a glass of rosé and looks like she actually enjoys it! They bring us dessert: a delicious chocolate cinnamon flan, which is their specialty. I notice Ingrid does not eat her whipped cream. I do.

We make a plan for tomorrow to go into Leon together, and then we will separate. Ingrid will be moving on from there, and I will stay an extra day to rest. I walk around the town alone after lunch, take some photos, and buy some snacks. I see Ingrid at one point, avoid her, and head back to my room for the night. I post on Facebook, read, eat the snacks, and doze off early.

I wake up to shouting in the street at midnight. Shouting…not as in fighting, just very loud talking. This is quite common in Spain. And then it starts...the cracks and sounds in my room, loud shifting and rustling. It definitely feels like I am not alone in here – this is the first time I have been a bit freaked out in a hotel room. So here I am writing at 2:00 a.m. I must try to sleep and surrender my fear. It's the old fear of being alone at night and feeling as if someone or something is "out to get me."

My Affirmations

I am safe. I am protected.
I am surrounded by divine white light.
God is always with me. God is always with me.
God is always with me.

Day Twenty-One

WALKING TO ARCAHUELA, 7 MILES/ 11.5 KM

"I don't live in either my past or my future. I'm interested only in the present. If you can concentrate always on the present, you'll be a happy man. Life will be a party for you, a grand festival because life is the moment we're living right now."

—Paulo Coelho

YESTERDAY, I ARRANGED TO MEET INGRID FOR BREAKFAST, walk halfway to Leon, and then taxi into the city. This is a big topic on the Camino, because getting into Leon involves walking on a busy highway and through an industrial zone. Even the guidebooks say this is a good part to skip. I know for sure I will skip it, and Ingrid is in agreement. We plan to share a cab once we get to Arcahuela, a small town outside of the city.

We start walking and take our time, speaking quietly, and I am quite enjoying her company. The tree-lined shady path is pleasant and off the highway, to begin with. As we continue on, the path turns right into the highway. Cars speed past us – the drivers seem lost in their own world, which is separate from ours. We can only walk single file, hugging the side of the road. I don't like it, at all. After a mile, or so, the way turns back into a wooded path again and we begin another conversation.

Gradually, I start to really resent Ingrid's voice. She talks about things I do not care about and do not want to hear. I crave my silence and would like to tell her, "Please be quiet. I don't want to hear anything more about your sister, her husband, their money, or their life. You judge them quite harshly. They're exactly where they need to be on their path. You are not superior to them."

But I hold my tongue. I do not think she would take kindly to my opinion, and we have only another mile or so to go. As we walk, my feet and legs become more tired, and I cannot help but think that if I were alone –saying my mantras, affirmations, and prayers – I would be feeling much better.

We make it to the town, cab it to Leon, and say our goodbyes. I am very happy to say, "Farewell, Buen Camino" to Ingrid from Holland now living in Spain. I feel like some past karma has been worked through and finished, and now it's on to the next phase!

I check into my hotel, another lovely restored monastery. I'm looking forward to today and a full rest day tomorrow. The room is very simple, nice and clean, on the second floor with a window that opens up to the busy street below. It has blackout shutters, which I am happy about, because I plan on getting a good, solid sleep. I shower and wash a few things and lay them on the open windowsill to dry. It is quite warm, about 85°, and this means my clothes will dry quickly. Note to myself: next Camino bring only quick dry clothing.

*"Faith is to believe what you do not see; the reward of this faith
is to see what you believe."*

—Saint Augustine

SAN FRANCISCO, CALIFORNIA: 1998

AFTER DECIDING TO LEAVE THE RANCH, I FIGURED THE
most logical step for my cooking career – now that I was
confident in my abilities – was to go back to the Bay Area.
My dream job was to cook at a winery and/or be a private
chef in Napa or the San Francisco area.

I packed up my belongings and my dogs and drove
north. My brother and his wife had recently purchased a
huge three-story house in the Marina district with views of
the Golden Gate Bridge and Alcatraz. It was an old house
that needed a complete renovation, but it was still livable.
They were living somewhere else for work and offered me
the house until I could get on my feet, or when they started
renovations.

So I lived in their huge house with my dogs, basically
taking over the main floor with a mattress, a few pieces of
furniture, and an old but working kitchen. I loved being
back in the Bay Area, and was enjoying bike riding and
walking a lot, especially on the marina green and dog beach
with the Golden Gate Bridge looming largely ahead.

I worked for a few different catering companies and
learned more about the business. At the same time, I was
working with a headhunter and seeking a private chef job. I
went on a few interviews/auditions with young wealthy families in Marin and Atherton, which are both affluent suburbs
of San Francisco. They seemed to like my cooking, and me

but the pay was ridiculously low, it was very expensive to live there and it just did not feel right.

After six months, the contractor for the house was hired, and I needed to move on. I drove to Napa to have a look, but it seemed like it would be difficult to find an affordable place to rent with my dogs. I found a house in Angwin, a small town about a fifteen-minute drive up Howell Mountain from St. Helena and the Silverado trail in the heart of the Napa Valley. I knew immediately that the house was meant for me when the owner informed that me she only rents to people with dogs!

Angwin is largely populated with Seventh Day Adventists because they have a college there. In this religion, alcohol is forbidden and they are strict vegetarians. There is only one small vegetarian market in the town, and as the local saying goes, "Just make sure you have your wine and your meat before you head up the hill!"

I ARRIVE IN LEON ON A SATURDAY. IT'S A BUSTLING SPANISH city filled with families: lots of children, parents, and grandparents. Families seem very close here and spend much quality time together. I find a nice outdoor café and order an aguacate salad. I never know quite what to expect when I order. I know aguacate is avocado and this is the first time I have seen it on a menu. I also order a glass of wine and sparkling water, which is brought to my table with a few pieces of bread resembling pizza, and a small plate of fried whole fish, probably sardines. The salad arrives, and here is a description of it: The plate is topped with thinly sliced tomatoes, sliced avocados, and sprinkled with corn. In between the avocado slices there are sliced pieces of chicken breast, and on top there is a plop of dressing resembling Thousand Island. There is also half of a hardboiled egg sitting in the dressing. It's an interesting dish, for sure. I enjoy it, especially the price. All this costs only about $10. As I eat, families begin to disappear, headed home for siesta, and it gets quieter. I walk around a bit, snap some photos, and head back to the hotel for my own siesta.

Later, I'm back out at 6:30 p.m. The sun is still very high and hot. I need to find a market to buy food. I'm going to stay in my room tonight and get to bed early, because the thought of eating alone in a big city restaurant makes me feel a bit down and lonely. I find a market and buy bread, hummus, water, wine, and vegetables escabeche, a type of vegetable salad marinated in a jar. I eat in my room while watching Jimmy Fallon and Ellen clips on YouTube, along with red wine, I enjoy my own company. I am smiling and happy.

Day Twenty-Two

"I prefer a kind of sweet, deep rich prayer in which a person goes in and says, 'take me down deep into the reason you gave me life. Take me down deep.' It silences the chaos in me."

—Caroline Myss

WAKING UP AND FEELING GOOD, I'M GRATEFUL FOR NINE hours of deep sleep! Something about these restored monasteries really agrees with me. My lesson today is a review. It's perfect for focusing on as I tour the city:

> *"God being love is also happiness. Let me remember love is happiness, and nothing else brings joy. And so I choose to entertain no substitute for love.*
> *"I seek what belongs to me in truth.*
> *"Love is my heritage and with it joy. These are the gifts my father gave to me. I would accept all that is mine in truth."*

—*A Course in Miracles*, Lesson 117

SO, ONCE AGAIN, I ASK FOR HELP IN REMOVING THAT which is held in my body and my mind, and keeps me from fully embracing the love, joy, and happiness that are mine, in truth. I forgive myself for believing that I am not worthy or deserving.

I mean, sure, I have had bouts of joy, happiness, and love, but it certainly has never lasted for very long. The sadness and seriousness always sets back in.

Here's the thing, as a young child I believed I was happy. I never really thought about it. But I was shy and sensitive, and when my parents started fighting night after night, and subsequently went through a horrible divorce, I realized there is much pain and sadness in this world. I just wanted to disappear and not cause any waves. I was always afraid to speak up, afraid of being rejected and criticized. This is what I learned from all the fighting going on around me, certainly not how to love others or follow the dreams of my heart.

NEWPORT BEACH, CALIFORNIA: 1977

THE FIRST TIME I GOT DRUNK WAS AT AGE FIFTEEN. I WAS drinking cheap whisky and beer and smoking bad weed, and ended up puking on the side of the road after a friend's party. That night, with the drugs and alcohol my shyness disappeared, and I liked it. At seventeen, I was raped. I thought I deserved it. I also believed the message that came along with it: do not look too good or too sexy, and do not be too friendly towards men because bad things will happen.

The morning after the rape, my mother yelled at me, demanding to know why I was not at school.

How could I tell her I had been up all night doing coke? And that I was driving home at 3:00 a.m. and was getting close to home, when my car started sputtering just as I was driving up the hill on Jamboree Rd?

I drove through a traffic light, made the left turn onto

Eastbluff Drive, and my car finally died – right in front of my high school. I didn't realize it at first, but there was a van following me. It stopped right behind me and a guy got out. He was around forty and large, with a bearded face. He walked up to my open window and said, "Oh, I did not realize you were so pretty. I saw your car and thought you might need some help. What are you doing out so late?"

I know it's stupid, but I was seventeen and high, so I told him, "I've been out partying."

"Doing what?"

Thinking I'm so cool, I said, like I was proud of it, "Oh… doing coke, drinking, smoking pot."

The man eyed me and said, "Well, I have some coke and I can give you a ride home."

At this point, I didn't know what to do. My car was dead, there was nobody around, and we were about a mile from my house. I was trusting, and he seemed sincere in his offer to help, so I agree to the ride home.

When I got into his van, he offered me a line of coke, which I accepted. He talked a bit and then he tried to kiss me. When I pulled away, he pushed me down onto a mattress in the back of the van. Frozen with fear, I tried to get away from him, but he was very strong and had no problem holding me down.

Finally, I just kind of surrendered and zoned out. I don't know how long it went on…several minutes, half an hour? When I opened my eyes, he was staring at me. Looking back at him, I said, "Please stop." Miraculously, he did, and then he drove me home.

How could I have told anyone about this? Like I said, I felt it was my own fault and I deserved it. I believed that if I told anyone I would be judged and criticized. There was so much partying and escapism going on at that time. I never really thought much more about it, but simply shoved it down along with all the other pain in my life.

I found a Thai massage place in Leon yesterday and made an appointment for 10:00 a.m. today, thinking I would give it another try. This time, a woman will do my massage. After breakfast, I head over. She starts out gently and then… BAM! She goes right to the same points on my legs. As I said before, "I love Thai massage," but maybe it's not so good in Spain on the Camino. However, to be honest, I feel calm and relaxed after she is finished.

As I make my way to the cathedral, a must see in Leon, the city is just starting to wake up. The Cathedral and plaza are breathtaking, a work of wonder. The cathedral itself is not open now, so I go to the museum next door. It's connected to the cathedral, and I'm told it was a cloister where the monks lived at one time. It is a beautiful outdoor space, and I walk around several times, marveling at the sacred architecture. I sit for a bit mesmerized by the amazing sculptures and spires of the church. Once again, I experience a sense of familiarity, belonging, and peace. I could sit here for hours in the stillness.

I wonder if this is all there is to the church and museum, although, certainly, this would have been enough. There are several locked doors and no one else is around, then a woman walks by. She appears to be a worker, so I ask her, "Todo?" meaning, "Is this everything?"

She leads me to a large wooden door without saying anything, unlocks it, brings me in, then leaves quickly and locks the door behind me from the outside!

Panic, claustrophobia, and fear set in. There is a stairway, but I can't see anyone else. I am confused and try to surrender my fear. I tell myself, I *am safe.* It's another experience of my ancient fear of being locked up and suffocation, I tell myself I'm safe over and over for several minutes. My heart is pounding and I don't know quite what to do. Finally the door opens again, another pilgrim enters, and my fear subsides.

Am I reliving one or more of my past lives? What the heck happened to me in those lives? And why do I still experience feelings related to them?

Looking around, I realize this is a three-story museum, and obviously it is kept locked. I walk upstairs and there are other people in there, as well. The Catholic paintings, sculptures, crosses, robes, and other clothing are fascinating, but it seems like almost everything is a depiction of pain and suffering, torture and power. No wonder so many people have bought into all of this and have so much fear and guilt.

I am happy to exit back out into the fresh air, ready for lunch and wine! My lunch includes: salad, veggie pizza, and ice cold, white wine. The food is tasty, and it's quite lovely to sit outside on the Plaza Isidoro. I feel mellow and content.

Back in my room for siesta, I check Facebook and see that Carey from San Diego is also in Leon. We make a plan to meet up later with her friend, who is arriving from California. On my way to meet them, I'm planning to stop at an ATM because I'm running low on cash. The first ATM gives me no cash…not working? I'm not sure, but the guy before me got cash. I go up the street to another ATM, and again, no cash. This is strange; maybe it's a busy Sunday and they ran out. Worry sets in, but I figure I can try again the following morning on my way out of town.

Visiting with Carey and her friend Erin is fun. We share a bottle of wine and tapas on the plaza and they tell stories of how they met, their kids, and their families. It's all quite pleasant, but a bit too much for me, so I opt to move on without them in favor of going back to my room and to bed early.

Day Twenty-Three

Walking to Villavante, 13 miles/21 km

"Find out who you are and be that person. That's what your soul was put on this earth to be. Find that truth, live that truth and everything else will come."

—Ellen DeGeneres

I DECIDE TO START A BIT LATER TODAY BECAUSE I NEED TO find a bank, and I want to cab it out of Leon through the ugly, industrial, first 4 miles. Even then, it will still be a 13-mile walk to Villavante.

I try a few ATMs, but it's a no go, and the banks are not open yet. Long story short, it turns out that my bank, which has been changed over to a new bank, sent me new ATM cards with instructions saying, "Please use these new cards because your present cards will no longer work." I understand this, but I informed the bank manager personally before I left that I would be in Spain for five weeks. "No problem," he said. "Your card will be fine."

However, I do not know this yet, because I am walking and cannot call my bank back in the states until it opens at 6 p.m. Spain time.

Well...if the fear of suffocation is bad, the fear of not

having cash and access to my money is even worse. The thoughts come flooding in: *Oh My God, all my money is gone; someone cleaned me out; how I will I get by with no cash? I will be abandoned and not able to get the things I need.* And, I have learned, no one in the small villages will take a credit card. On and on goes my mind, fearful over having no money, never enough money, freaking out, big fear, no money!

Maybe I can get a cash advance on my credit card, but I don't know if it will work here in Spain. My mind continues to freak out – not to mention that I am very upset with the bank. I realize how ridiculous my fears are, but I cannot let them go.

So I pray and chant one of my favorite Sanskrit verses from the *Guru Gita*, which is chanted in its entirety every morning in Siddha Yoga ashrams and centers around the world:

Om purnamadah purnamidam
Om, that is perfect.
Purnat purnamudacyate
This is perfect.
Purnasya purnamadaya
From the perfect springs the perfect.
Purnamevavasisyate
If the perfect is taken from the perfect, the perfect remains.
Om shanti, shanti, shanti
Om, Peace, peace, peace.

I REPEAT THIS CHANT OVER AND OVER, HAVING FAITH THAT it is going to work, until my mind finally quiets and once again my only concern is walking and getting to Villavante. (This stuff really works!)

I make it about halfway, stop for a brief rest, and order

an Aquarius, Europe's equivalent to Gatorade. The next part of the way is on the road, which means hard pavement. As I continue to walk, my feet and legs begin to hurt and burn. I am on the road with noisy trucks and cars and tractors flying by me and I am not happy. *What the hell am I doing; this is torture!*

I am trying to be kind to myself and remember to love myself – no torture, no struggle, listen to my body – but at this point there's not much I can do but keep on walking. I see an intersection ahead, crossing over the pavement where the Camino turns into a dirt path. My feet are screaming, so I stop and change into my sandals and try calling the hotel for a pick-up. My paperwork stated they would come and pick me up, if needed. No one answers the phone. I sit and keep trying for thirty minutes…still no answer. I walk on, feeling a bit better for a while with the change of shoes, until the pain and tiredness starts again and the anger comes. It has been simmering, but now it is at a full boil and I explode:

"What the f__k! Is there anyone out there? Someone, please help me*!* I am so f__king over this, over this world, over this pain, over the suffering. I release all of this crap! I want it out, finished. How many times do I have to ask? I am innocent, NO MORE PAIN, no more pain, sadness and false beliefs about myself. I know the strength is in me and I need it now!" By this time, I am shouting and ready to break a tooth from gritting my teeth so hard. As I scream into the wind, there is no one to hear me except the birds and the butterflies, who are gently, lovingly flying all around me as though they want to help. The tears come lightly, at first, I let go and the floodgates open. I walk into the town sobbing.

Of course, the inn is at the end of town, so I keep

walking – or I should say "hobbling and crying like a lame duck," not caring who sees me. I call again, and finally the innkeeper answers and comes to pick me up. I am only about four blocks away, but I can hardly step into the van. I'm fairly certain she recognizes and feels my pain.

Getting to the inn, the magic begins. Mercedes, the owner, is so kind and caring. She sits me down and brings me fresh cherries from her tree, nuts, and an ice-cold beer. There is no one else around, and she asks how my day is going. When I tell her about my trouble with the bankcards, she goes and gets her credit card machine and tries my cards. The first one is declined, so she tries my Chase card for five euros and it goes through. When she hands me a five-euro bill, I almost start crying with relief. She actually offers to loan me cash – she will give me her bank account number and I can deposit the loan back into her account in Sarria (which is five days away) when I get my money. Her sweet, genuine offer is overwhelming. I tell her, "If that is the case, can you just charge my card now that we know its working. Add your percentage so it doesn't cost you anything." She says, "Okay, no problem, talk later, you go rest."

The room is lovely, a sweet comfortable country inn room with views of the lush countryside and gardens filled with lavender, fruit trees, and colorful flowers. Now it's time to shower, put my legs up the wall, stretch, and rest.

At 6:00 p.m., I call my bank, and sure enough the cards were canceled due to the bank change. The bank manager says, "But we sent you new cards; didn't you receive them?"

"Well obviously not before my trip; remember the one I informed you about?"

"Oh my God. I am so sorry." He didn't know what else

to say. The ATM card I have in hand cannot be reinstated, so he offers to send my new card. I agree and arrange with Marti, a friend who is taking care of my home and my dogs, to bring it into the bank. He will activate the new card and send it to me in Spain via FedEx. This still means I will not have access to my bank account for a week.

In the meantime, I call Chase about getting a cash advance on my credit card the following day in Astoria.

"Hold on, we need to transfer you to our fraud department. Did you make an online purchase yesterday for riding equipment and other things?"

Surprised, I answer, "No."

"Evidentially, your card has been compromised. We will send out a new one."

"No, I need to use my card right now."

I explain my situation and they agree to let me use the card for in-person purchases while in Spain.

"Okay, great," the fraud department person says. "But do not charge anything over the Internet and no cash advance."

No problem. I go to dinner and Mercedes offers once again to give me cash on my credit card as a cash advance. She puts in for €100 and it is declined.

"Please may I have a glass…or make it a bottle…of wine, while I go call the bank again."

At this point, to say I'm frustrated is an understatement! Back on the phone with Chase, I attempt to explain the whole thing again. Finally, they guarantee that my card will work in Spain.

"Please try your transaction again."

We do, the transaction goes through, and Mercedes hands me €100. A nice dinner follows, with us sharing pictures of family. After dinner, Mercedes takes me on a tour of the inn, which is quite lovely, only eight rooms. I am the only person staying here tonight, even though the previous nights have been fully booked. I tell Mercedes she is my Camino Angel.

Day Twenty-Four

WALKING TO ASTORGA, 11 MILES/ 18 KM

"And the day came when the risk to remain in a tight bud was more painful than the risk it took to bloom."

—Anais Nin

AFTER A GREAT SLEEP, I WAKE UP WITH A FEELING OF DREAD about walking today. I am worried about my feet, especially after hearing about my friend Craig, who took two days off to ice his shin splints, felt great, and started walking again. He only made it about 4 miles before he had to stop on the side of the trail, while Heather went to find someone to pick him up. They are now taking a train to Leon for three more days of ice and rest – it does not sound good.

Getting to Astorga means a relatively short walk today, only 11 miles, and it does look like there are quite a few places for rest and to call a cab, if needed. After breakfast, I give Mercedes a big hug and leave. I guess it rained during the night, although I heard nothing, it is wet and cloudy this morning. I see a few pilgrims up ahead, but I am walking quite slowly, babying my feet. Before I realize it, no one else is ahead of me and no one is behind. My feet are hurting, and I'm thinking: *Maybe when I get to the first town I will rest and take a cab.*

Beginning again, I repeat this affirmation: *There is no pain and no suffering in God.*

I come to a fork in the road, and the Camino markers point both ways. It looks like the left might be quieter, so I choose to go left. The path seems to be heading towards some sort of large industrial plant, and this is not a welcome sight. I start feeling uneasy, because there is no one in sight. Fear comes over me, but I keep walking and surrendering the fear with affirmations, as I pass the noisy, bad vibes power plant filled with huge mechanical monsters.

I am safe. I am protected. I offer everyone peace of mind. The thought: *What the hell am I doing,* arises in my mind, once again. I want to be safe, feel safe, and enjoy life.

Finally, I see the street and head towards the town. A simple smile and "Buen Camino" from a local woman has me in tears, and the tears come again as I walk through the town. I see a few pilgrims up ahead and as I turn the corner am rewarded with a magnificent view of a cobblestone street leading to an ancient stone bridge over the river Orbigo. Here is the town with the bars and the pilgrims.

I realize that when I was afraid a while back, the pain in my foot mostly disappeared. I suppose when you're in pain it's hard to focus on anything else, so it seems the fear overrides the pain. It seems that if we could just focus on the highest love, we would have no pain or fear. I walk on and choose the trail marked a bit shorter, but near the highway. I find out later that the other path is only about a half mile longer and it's quiet and lovely. Oh well. As I walk today, I am thinking of my family and missing them. I realize I have held on to many unresolved conflicts, and blamed them and others for my beliefs about myself. Blaming gives me an excuse for not being fully alive and holding myself back, and in the process I have withheld love and shut down. I have been searching for years, trying to open and let go, and love myself….but still I am not free.

My Prayer

Mother, father, God, Goddess, please help me open to love, to share love, to be loved, to let go, to forgive others, and especially to forgive myself.

Napa, 1999

I KNEW SOMEONE WHO WORKED IN SALES AT CAIN VINE-yard and Winery. He got me in to do a few private dinners; they liked me and asked if I wanted to cook for the upcoming harvest season. As is the French custom, the winery provides a bountiful lunch for staff and visitors during this busy time of picking grapes at the peak of ripeness and the start of the wine making process.

I jumped at the chance, this being one of my dream jobs: chef at a winery. The job entailed three lunches per week for 25 – 40 people, with days in-between for shopping and prep. I took requests from the staff and was able to get very creative, especially with all of the amazing artisan and organic products available in the area. Artisan food producers and winemakers are some of the most passionate people I have met, and you can definitely taste the love in the finished products.

Cain is a beautiful, majestic winery known for its highly rated Bordeaux-style red blends. It is hidden away on Spring Mountain, on the other side of the valley from Angwin. The setting is stunning: acres and acres of vineyards on steep slopes, lush gardens, and breathtaking views. I loved my early misty morning drives down Howell Mountain and back up Spring Mountain, which is filled with oak, fig, and eucalyptus trees, acres of vineyards and wineries hidden among the windy road and dense forest. Not to mention the distinct smell of fermentation was in the air, which added to this special season. I loved my time at Cain, but harvest season lasts only two and a half months, and when it ended I still did not have a full-time cooking position at Cain or anywhere else.

Gurumayi was going to be in Ontario, CA for the 1999–2000 two-week New Year's retreat (only an hour drive from my mom's in Rancho Mirage, near Palm Springs) so I drove down and offered to do cooking seva. It is always a joy to see old seva/ SYDA friends, catch up, and be of service to the Guru with the many thousands of devotees coming from all over the world to chant, meditate, study, and be immersed in the Shakti, the spiritual energy that fills the environment. Of course, they all needed to be fed!

While there, it became clear that I was meant to move back to the Palm Springs area and create my own catering business, which had been my long-held dream. My father, who was also in the area, offered me and my dogs a place to live until I got settled and on my feet. This turned out to be a great blessing as he passed away a few years later.

My business started slowly, at a nice pace allowing me to learn from my mistakes and successes. I was invited back to Cain for 2 more harvest seasons and a few months in the summer back at the ranch. It all worked out perfectly and I was grateful.

As I walk towards Astorga, I pass many younger pilgrims I haven't seen before. The pilgrims I became familiar with earlier are ahead of me now, and I see new faces. I come to the outskirts of Astorga and stop at a bar for an Aquarius and a snack. I contemplate a cab and as I rest, the owner and his friend sit next to me, and we communicate in our broken languages. They are very sweet and wish me "Buen Camino." I feel like their well wishes are a blessing and I decide to keep walking.

My hotel tonight is located on one of the town plazas. I shower, rest, and go out to find a bank, a market, and the start of the Camino for tomorrow. However, it's 3:00 p.m., siesta time, and everything is closed. So I walk to the Cathedral and the Episcopal Palace, a beautiful building designed by the famous architect Gaudi.

Back in my room, I read, write, and stretch, and wait for dinner. At 6:30, I head downstairs because this restaurant serves straight through. The bartender looks at me like I am nuts when I say I want to eat. "NOW?" he asks incredulously. "Yes, I am very tired, muy consado," I say, because, as we know by now, most Spaniards eat dinner around 9:00 p.m.

He relents and brings me a typical pilgrim meal of insalata mista, roast chicken with potatoes, and white wine. I notice a guy I had seen on the trail earlier, and as he finishes his beer he announces he also wants to eat – again, annoying the bartender. They set him up at a table next to mine. He is David from France, in his early 30s. We chat for a bit and he invites me to sit with him. He is a traveler who works periodically and saves money to get to his next destination. He totally trusts in the universe and his intuition to lead and support him. And it always, *always* works. David's next goals are Australia and the U.S. He asks a lot of questions and says he would like to go to San Diego. He will walk the Camino for seven more days, go home for a month to work, and buy a one-way ticket to San Diego. Maybe we will keep in touch, maybe not, but I am pretty sure he will be happy and do well in life.

Day Twenty-Five

"Appreciation and self-love are the most important aspects you could ever nurture. Appreciation of others and the appreciation of yourself are the closet vibrational matches to Source energy of anything we have ever witnessed in this universe."

—Abraham-Hicks

After a good sleep and breakfast, I'm out the door at 7:11 a.m. The first part of the walk is really pleasant and I feel great – the crisp morning air is so refreshing on my skin. There are many pilgrims on the road and I feel quite safe. This is the area where Denise, a pilgrim who has been missing for 6 weeks and is the talk of the Camino, was last seen, and it is advised not to walk alone here. Today's destination is about 13 miles away. I am hoping to make it without pain in my legs and feet.

My ACIM review lesson today is so simple, the key to everything. I could use these affirmations forever. Try it. Simply close your eyes, place your hand over your heart, and repeat a few times, "I rest in God." This simple statement brings me to peace every time.

"I rest in God today and let Him work in me and through me while I rest in Him in quiet and in perfect certainty.

I am as God created me. I am God's son [or daughter]. Today I lay aside all sick illusions of myself and let my Father tell me what I really am."

—*A Course in Miracles,* Lesson 120

AS I WALK AND REPEAT THESE LESSONS, THE FIRST PART of the path becomes narrow and I am only able to walk single file. Surrounded by several other pilgrims, I see many new faces passing me. Some of them come right up behind me, which really bugs me. I'd like to tell them, "If you want to pass, please say something; a simple smile and "Buen Camino" will do. Some are trailing me, right on my ass, until I step aside and let them pass – without a word from them. I try to smile and say, "Buen Camino." Oh, forgiveness lessons come from everywhere. Thank you. Thank you!

Passing through a small, crumbling down village, the only signs of life are at the Camino Cowboy bar, a funky little place that looks like a converted garage. Resting here for an apple and an Aquarius, I enjoy watching the pilgrims and listening to a local man standing on the curb who is singing and playing guitar. I snap some photos and head out, figuring I only have about four miles to go. It is warming up as I pass a large tourist bus parked on the side of the road. Next to the bus, a group of about thirty pilgrims are lacing up for their short walk today. I believe I will see more and more of this as I get closer to Santiago. They are very friendly and wish me well as I pass.

As I wind my way along the path, out of nowhere a young boy with a beautiful, bright smile, around ten, is selling cherries packed in homemade newspaper cones. I cannot resist buying some. For 1 euro, they are the best cherries I have ever eaten.

Continuing on, hot and tired, I really start to slow down, but I press on knowing there are only about 2 miles to go. I see a van on the side of the road with coolers and a couple of locals who are selling cold drinks. I approach, stop, and ponder whether I should rest a few minutes or push on. A woman sees me and offers me a chair, "Come peregrina, come sit and rest." I gladly accept her offer and buy cold water, to which I add Emergen-C. Taking off my shoes and giving myself a foot rub, I change into sandals.

David from last night passes by, gives me the European kiss on each cheek, and says. "Let's meet up for a drink later." I rest a few more minutes and walk on. It seems like everything gets more difficult when I know the destination is so close. Pain and fatigue set in from walking on a slight ascent on hot asphalt. Two more miles to go.

All I can say to myself, over and over, is: *God is walking through me. God walks through me. I rest in God. I am as God created me,* and *God take over.* This takes me out of my head, and it works – it always works.

"When you trust that whatever you have to go through, the Beloved is with you, showering you with grace and the deepest, most tender compassion, you do not cease to suffer. But instead of being defeated or paralyzed by your suffering, you realize it has profound meaning, and slowly, you trust more and more that that meaning will be revealed to you."

—Andrew Harvey

Slowly making it to Rabanal, I arrive tired and hungry. The hotel for tonight is at the end of town – which means another hill to walk up – and I'm already hot, sweaty, and cranky. The guy who checks me in could not be any less friendly and indifferent. I smile, say "thank you," and ask about food.

"1-3 for lunch," he says in a curt voice. I do not think this man likes women, or maybe he just doesn't like American women who are walking the Camino, or maybe he is the perfect mirror of my crankiness.

I contemplate my luggage and the three flights of stairs. UGGH! Obviously, I will not be getting any help from this guy. Looking up the stairs, I see a lady cleaning the rooms. She sees me and immediately comes down, grabs my luggage, and leads me to my room. She is another Camino Angel. Muchas Gracias! This Camino really teaches a person to be grateful for simple kindness.

My room is quite spacious and feels really good. I open the curtains and am happily surprised to see a double door opening to a small balcony with a clothesline and a beautiful expansive view of the countryside. Okay, this makes up for the guy at the desk. My hips and feet are throbbing, so I do my usual routine: shower, stretch, legs up the wall.

I head down for lunch and am the only one in the dining room. The woman working there must be the guy's daughter because they have the same personality. Oh well… I just want to eat. The pilgrim meal is a salad, grilled salmon (that's a new one), and French fries. The house rosé tastes like mold, so it sits there untouched. I order a sparkling water and guzzle it down.

After eating, I head back up for more rest. I am feeling a bit down and lonely again – like I am ready for the walking to be over and I'm missing my dogs, my home, and my bed.

I need to get out and see the town and buy some snacks for dinner, and maybe run into David for that drink. Coming to the town church, there is a caretaker outside and I ask, "Abierto? Open?" "Si Si, yes yes," he says, with a kind smile as he opens the door for me. There is nobody else in this small church. As the door closes behind me, I instinctively put my hand over my heart. The atmosphere is simple, austere, and profound. The power in this small church frightens me, humbles me, and grounds me. Immediately, the tears come, as I sit, look around in awe and wonder, and repeat: *I rest in God. I am as God created me. I let go of the sick illusions I have made up about myself. I am here to serve. Divine guidance, Please lead the way.*

Leaving the church with a new sense of peace and renewal, I pass an Albergue where people are talking and laughing. Maybe I should go in and join them, but I don't feel comfortable doing this. My shyness and insecurities hold me back. After buying snacks, I am back in my room for the night, feeling lonely and starting to get angry because the open windows are inviting in many flies. I say to them, "You better leave! I am in the mood to smash something and you will be it." I grab a towel and start swinging it trying to remove the flies. I tell them, "I warned you," and then I smash a few, releasing the anger bubbling up inside of me. I feel pain and loneliness, and I am ashamed of my anger. Where does all this come from? I let it come and collapse in exhaustion.

Later, I post a few photos on Facebook and tell my friends, "Everything is getting harder the closer I get to Santiago." The comments come in quickly, "You can do it! You got this! Power and peace to you!" Overwhelmed with their support and love, I cry myself to sleep.

Day Twenty-Six

*"Holding onto anger is like grasping a hot coal with
the intent of throwing it at someone else; you are the one
who gets burned."*

—Buddha

*"The truth in you remains as radiant as a star, as pure as light,
as innocent as love itself."*

—*A Course in Miracles*

I AWAKE TO THE SOUND OF BIRDS SINGING – THE FLIES I did not smash last night also wake up. I am ready for the day, knowing it will be a long day and it will be warm. I have a quick breakfast, and after thinking about the check-in guy and my forgiveness opportunity, I send him love and light. He checks me out, gives me directions, and now seems like a sweet, little, old man.

I thank him and hit the trail. It's an uphill climb for 2 miles on a narrow windy path. There is no one else that I can see on the Camino right now, and surprisingly I feel really good. I repeat my mantra continuing to walk at a good pace: *God is... I forgive. God is...I forgive*

Cruz de Ferro is a stopping point signified by a simple iron cross where pilgrims lay a rock or other token as a symbol of letting go of something, a prayer or blessing. Before leaving home, a friend gave me a few small stones to carry with me. I chose to leave them here. Actually, this entire journey has been a blessing and a letting go, so I did not feel much at Cruz de Ferro when I released my stones.

Continuing on, I thank my body, my feet, and my legs for supporting me. I feel like I've definitely gotten stronger and maybe lost a few pounds. It's hard to tell because all of my clothes are loose fitting. I did not want to make this journey about losing weight, but more about accepting myself. Of course, I secretly hoped I would drop some pounds, but I need the food and the carbs to keep me going, and, of course, the wine helps at the end of the day. I have spoken to several women who are using the Camino as a crash diet, not that they put it this way. For example, one says, "I eat breakfast, then a large salad for lunch, and then try not to eat dinner, but just drink wine. I want to drop at least 15 pounds." I personally do not know how you can eat so little while hiking all day, day after day. And what is going to happen when you get back home to your husband and your kids? How are you going to maintain your weight loss? As with all crash diets, I believe you won't! So what is the point in messing with your metabolism? Well, this is only my opinion. To each his or her own – it's their Camino.

The path flattens out for a bit, but then the rocky, uneven downhill starts. I don't know how the other pilgrims are walking by so quickly. They almost seem to be running! I need to really take my time and enjoy the mountainous views, knowing more injuries happen on the downhill. I make my way slowly to Acebo and wander around the charming small town, stop at a bar, look at the route, and call a cab. Having already walked over 11 miles today – and it looks like more downhill on asphalt – I decide to get help.

Here is the funny part. The cab ride that was supposed to make this easier is one of the scariest experiences on the Camino, so far. The guy is friendly, too friendly. He's not watching the road, and it is a narrow, curvy, downhill, two-lane highway with no guardrails. He is talking into his phone translator trying to talk to me. Yikes! Seriously, he almost goes off the side of the road, over-corrects, and barely misses another car coming head on.

"Dude! Watch the road!" I shout, but he only laughs, "Ha, ha. No problema."

Making it to my hotel in one piece, I am given another comfortable, quiet room with great air-conditioning. Surprise, surprise! I am hungry and the hotel restaurant menu looks easy and good. There are only a handful of other diners, so I choose to sit at a central table. I don't know why, because I usually choose a corner or back table when dining alone. There is a local couple sitting near me, and the woman keeps staring at me with what seems to be disapproval. Is it wrong or somehow bad in this culture for women to travel alone? Possibly. I have had many looks like this from the local women. I do my best to ignore it, send her a nice smile, enjoy lunch, and then I head out to find a market and a bank.

While walking around, I pass the large Templar Castle, built in the eleventh century to defend the road to Santiago. It is quite stunning, and if I had more energy I might walk over and take a tour. But I am just not in the mood. I look around town, find an open market, buy some snacks, find an ATM, and pray that my American Express card will work for a one-time cash advance. I hold my breath…. hooray, thank you Amex. Now I can feel good about my money situation until I arrive in Sarria, where my new bankcard should be waiting for me at the hotel. Snacks, Ellen, Jimmy Fallon, and I'm off to bed.

Day Twenty-Seven

"Don't believe what your eyes are telling you. All they show is limitation. Look with your understanding, find out what you already know and you'll see the way to fly."

—Richard Bach

I HEAD OUT EARLY AGAIN, KNOWING IT IS GOING TO BE blazing hot. I would like to make it to town as early as possible. The first part of the walk is through town and mostly industrial. I probably could've skipped it. As I get through the city, it starts to become quiet, and for several miles I walk through many small towns with beautiful gardens and friendly locals. I make it easily to the town of Cacabelos, a quaint, lively town known for the local wines. After walking through many vineyards and bodegas, (wineries) I am anxious to try the wine. I still have several miles to go, and it is only 10:00 a.m., so I stop and order only an Aquarius, knowing I will sample the wine later.

Walking out of town, I start to feel a blockage in my chest and it's hard to catch my breath. I know something old is stuck there, some fear or trauma keeping me from freedom of breath. I also feel a bit dizzy. Seeing some park benches, I stop to rest. A woman from Canada, Joanne, comes up and sits with me. She has just started her Camino, and is very enthusiastic and friendly. I tell her what's going on, and she offers great support by talking with me. It's amazing how the Camino always provides exactly what is needed at the right moment. We walk together to the next town, where she is scheduled to stay for the day. I thank her and wish her "Buen Camino."

The walking gets more difficult as the sun gets higher. The asphalt feels like a pancake griddle and I am the pancake getting fried! Some uphill highway walking leads to miles of vineyards. Usually I love walking through vineyards, but I am ready to be done walking. The pain in my feet is returning, my legs ache, and sweat is running down my face. Thinking I will never arrive, relief washes over me as I round a corner and get the first glimpses of Villafranca. I must say, it is stunning, and it helps get my mind off the pain in my feet.

Finding my hotel in the maze of streets is difficult, requiring me to walk several more kilometers, feeling each step. When I arrive, the owner of the inn says in a somewhat angry voice, "Rooms not ready until 2. You can leave your backpack here if you want."

After sitting for a moment, I leave in search of an open bar and a cold beer. I find one on a quiet side street and ask the woman behind the bar for *comida* (food), she looks at me as if I am an alien because it is only 12:30. She offers me a bag of potato chips.

Anne from Norway, whom I met on the trail earlier, comes in and joins me. She only has four more days to get to Santiago, so she must decide which parts to skip.

We talk about tomorrow, which consists of a very difficult, 18-mile walk along the highway, followed by a steep ascent to O'Cebreio. She decides to skip it, and at this point so do I. After much worrying about the upcoming 18-mile trek with throbbing and swollen feet, I decide tomorrow will be a rest day. There is only one bus, and it leaves at 5:30 a.m., so I decide on a taxi. The owner of the hotel will arrange it.

My room here is quite lovely and spacious, with a large bed, bathroom, and double doors opening out onto a small balcony and the cobblestoned street below. I immediately roll out my yoga mat, do some stretches, and put my legs up the wall. Dozing off in this position, I completely let go of the day's events.

Alone in the small dining room for dinner, I order a local wine, which is delicious, and am served a simple salad of tomatoes and roasted peppers drizzled with a tasty vinaigrette. This is followed by a chunky chicken stew. It is quite delicious and satisfying. The owner seems nicer now. He brings me a homemade coffee flan for dessert with a smile on his face – it's the first smile I've seen from him – and I gladly devour the flan. All through dinner, "The Best of Sting" plays on his computer. Leaving, I compliment him on the food and music selection.

As I settle in for the night, I feel lonely. Why do I isolate myself and create such loneliness? I have heard about the Albergues and the community available there. In some, you can book private rooms or double rooms, and now I realize they may not have been as horrible as I had first thought.

I think of my family and friends and miss them. I turn on Facebook and learn that the Supreme Court has legalized gay marriage in all fifty states. This is great news, and

I cry with joy as I imagine the love and celebrating happening back in the states, especially with my friends in San Francisco. I post a big Hooray on Facebook and send love from the Camino!

Day Twenty-Eight

"The trick is in what one emphasizes.
We either make ourselves miserable, or we make ourselves happy.
The amount of work is the same."

—Carlos Castaneda

I WAKE UP THIS MORNING TO AN EMAIL FROM MY MOM. SHE sends a cute photo of herself and a friend, and writes that she misses me and is sad that I am not there. She is thinking of me every minute of every day. I cry and think about how I have partly blamed her for my body issues. I cry and forgive her and forgive myself, and plan on creating much love between us in the future. There have been so many gifts that I denied because I was stuck in my ego, stubborn, and in negativity. I accept them now and am determined to give as much as I can in return.

My lesson today is thankfulness: "I thank my Father for His gifts to me."

"Today in gratitude we lift our hearts above despair, and raise our thankful eyes, no longer looking downward to the dust. We sing the song of thankfulness today, in honor of the Self that God has willed to be our true identity in Him. Today we smile on everyone we see, and walk with lightened footsteps as we go to do what is appointed us to do."

—*A Course in Miracles,* Lesson 123

A TAXI IS COMING FOR ME AT 9:45 A.M., I HEAD DOWN TO the lobby at 9:30. In walks a couple with Steffi from Russia, a woman I met yesterday. Steffi has serious blisters on her feet, but she started walking this morning anyway. She had so much pain from the blisters that she was limping along slowly and wondering how she was going to accomplish the difficult day ahead!

The couple noticed her and invited her to sit with them for coffee. They are taking a cab today, also because of injuries, and they invite Steffi to join them. This couple also stayed here last night.

They are traveling with a larger group and a Shaman guy, and are on a spiritual journey, or so they tell me. Their group went on ahead today and they are taking a cab because of their blisters and shin splints. They reiterate the fact that the inn and rooms are very nice, but the owner is an asshole. They are convinced that he went into their room and stole money while they were out. I have no idea if this is true, but they say they are going to "ream" him on reviews and social media. I did not tell them this behavior is not very spiritual. I cannot help but think of my lesson: *Be thankful for ALL people.* There is always a lesson, a blessing there.

My cab arrives first and I am informed it is only a fifteen-minute ride for thirty-five euros. This is pretty steep, but what can I say. The drive on the highway is lovely, very mountainous and surrounded by much greenery and wildflowers. I pay the cabdriver and find my accommodations easily, as O'Cebreio is a very small, quaint village. It's on the highway and there are many large tour buses pulling in. The town has only a few hotels, bars, and souvenir shops.

The church in O'Cebreio is one of the earliest surviving buildings on the Camino, dating back to the ninth century! The interior is simple and welcoming. The big majestic cathedrals are awe-inspiring, but the simple humble churches are very powerful and peaceful. I sit for a few minutes and thank God for all the blessings in my life, and ask again to please remove that which blocks me from true love, joy, and happiness. I want to live in this state and embody the truth.

Later, sitting at a cafe with a shaded table and ordering a café con leche, I see Steffi, who joins me along with a few of her friends. They are guys in their early thirties from France and Sweden, and they have just arrived after walking the 18-mile route today. They left at 5:00 a.m. It is now about 11:00 a.m., which means it took these guys, who are in really good shape, six hours. They must move quickly, because if I had done the same walk it would have taken me at least nine hours. They are exhilarated and say it was beautiful and difficult, but they would not have missed it. One guy says it is his favorite day on the Camino, so far, and he feels like crying because he feels so blessed that he was able to do it.

After hearing this, I feel somewhat sad that I missed it, but I know I made the right decision because my feet are hurting just from walking around town on the cobblestone streets. I do miss walking on the days I take off to rest, and I look forward to walking the rest of the way to Santiago.

Sending my feet, legs and hips, and my entire body lots of love, energy, and healing, I repeat today's affirmation:

I am grateful for my beautiful strong body and I completely accept myself as I am.

Day Twenty-Nine

WALKING TO TRIACASTELA, 12.9 MILES/21 KM

"Your worth is not established by anything you say or do.
Your worth is established by God. Period. There is no room for
argument or discussion here. You are whole and perfect.
It doesn't matter what you think. God established your worth.
He created you perfect. Everything else is your own nightmare."

—Lisa Natoli

AFTER A NOT-SO-GREAT NIGHT OF TOSSING AND TURNING, I'm up early. After some light yoga, coffee, and toast, I'm on the road at 6:30 a.m. I choose a path out of town that is shown in my guidebook, but, in reality, not well marked. Completely alone again, I pray that this is actually the Camino and I am not lost. Listening to my intuition, it tells me to keep going. The morning is quiet and cool, a bit misty, and absolutely beautiful looking out over the valley below. I come to a "T" in the path and finally see a marker. Thank you! There are three pilgrims at the same place, and it seems amazing how they just appear seemingly out of nowhere. Seeing them is always a welcome sight.

According to the guidebook, it will be a relatively flat walk, and then downhill into Triacastela. I guess they must have thrown in these very steep inclines after the book was written! After making it to the top – I can only assume it's the top – I am dripping sweat. A welcome bar awaits me, and I order an Aquarius and down it. The temperature is quickly rising, so I keep going and hit the flat plateau for several miles. Thankfully, the path is tree-lined and mostly shaded. I continue with my mantras, thank my feet and body, and ask the Divine to take over.

My stomach starts to growl, I stop for a quick bite: a classic Spanish tortilla, also known as a potato frittata. YUM! It is perfect and hits the spot. Continuing to walk, soon I hit the last downhill miles and it's an open path with expansive views of green rolling hills and far-off villages. My rock star feet are starting to hurt. I send them love and figure it is about another hour of walking. I've got this. When I arrive at the outskirts of the next town and find out it's another two miles to the hotel, I walk slowly and methodically. I'm looking forward to a quiet rest in my room, a shower, and a nice lunch.

I find my hotel, which is actually a complex that includes an Albergue, a pensione, and a restaurant. The girl who checks me in is sweet and welcoming. She takes my suitcase and walks me down the street to where I will be staying, smiling all the way. We come to a bar and the barkeep takes my luggage and carries it, as he leads me to my room, which is three flights up. He is smiling and friendly the whole way. I think about how friendly people can be, and also the opposite, and hope more people will get it. This is your life and you get what you give. He is a perfect example that welcoming and kindness supersede most everything else. I feel very happy to be in this town.

The restaurant is full for lunch and the servers and bartenders are very busy with demanding, hungry, thirsty pilgrims. The entire staff is friendly while having fun with each other and the customers. I have a nice lunch, and then go back to the same restaurant for dinner, sit inside, and watch the scene unfold around me. I'm so impressed because even though they are very busy, they maintain a great attitude with beautiful smiles all while giving outstanding service.

Having been in the restaurant business for so many years, I am impressed, because I know how difficult this can be. They are Camino magic.

Day Thirty

WALKING TO SARRIA, 15.5 MILES/25 KM

"If you accept full responsibility for your life, you'll accept that your destiny is created by you, and your life is basically a symbol of your innermost thoughts and feelings of what you believe about yourself."

—Stuart Wilde

IT IS DAY THIRTY OF MY CAMINO AND ABOUT 15 MILES TO Sarria, which signifies the last hundred kilometers until Santiago. I slept fairly well last night, but woke up to aching feet, hips, and back. Only six more days of this strain on my body. My body aches but I feel strong and proud of myself for making it this far.

I have an early breakfast of café con leche, OJ, and a croissant. No protein offered here; caffeine and sugar will have to be my fuel this morning. The forecast is hot, in the 90s again. I check my guidebook and see there are two routes to choose from today. Of course, I want the shortest but somehow end up on the longest. This is confirmed by two girls I meet along the way, "Yes, it is longer, but flatter and much nicer."

I continue following the narrow path, with the highway on one side and a steep drop into the river on the other. If I

134   Jennifer Winn Johnson

trip and fall off the cliff, no one would ever find me. Maybe this is what happened to Denise, the missing pilgrim.

After about a mile like this, the path finally veers off the highway and into a wide-open, grassy, country path. I come to a short bridge and am mesmerized by the rushing water, which is loud and powerful and surrounded by yellow and red wildflowers and huge purple hydrangeas. As I am taking photos, a group of five comes up behind me. We chat a bit and start walking again. The group splits and I stay with Raphael, a friendly guy from Spain who is now living in Switzerland. He says he wants to walk with me so he can practice his English. Great, I could use some company today. Raphael's English is very good. He is sixty, recently retired, and has a wife back home. He has always wanted to walk the Camino.

We walk a few miles, alternating between words and silence. The path is quite lovely, very tranquil and quiet, and lined with giant trees that provide much-appreciated shade. There are no other pilgrims in sight. We agree this is definitely the better route. We come to a hill, walking quietly and breathing deeply. When we reach the top, we stop to rest for a few minutes and catch our breath. The decline is steep and rocky, not my favorite. I take it slowly and carefully, my walking sticks my constant companions. I make a comment about how the downhill is harder and hurts my feet more.

"It is because you are heavy," Raphael says, so matter-of-factly in his heavily accented English. It stops me in my tracks. I am confused and think I must have misunderstood, something lost in translation. Nobody, a stranger much less a fellow pilgrim, would ever say such a thing to someone they had just met. I'm so surprised by his comment that I say nothing.

We walk together in silence for several more miles, enjoying the beautiful serene path. We arrive in the town of Samos, which is known for its stunning Benedictine monastery. Founded in the sixth century as a school for theology and philosophy, it is still active today. There's a café across the street from the monastery, and Raphael's friends are already seated at a table outside. It is definitely time for a break.

Raphael asks about my feet and suggests I take my shoes off and rest. "You are heavy and you need to reduce so your feet will not hurt so much." This time there's no mistaking it. He's calling me heavy, and I'm shocked and dumbfounded.

I have actually been feeling much better about my body and myself here on the Camino. But BAM! One comment and all the pain and hurt come rushing to the surface. I'm certainly not going to let him see me cry. I go to the bathroom, bury my face in my hands, and sob.

I weep for the little girl who never felt loved during her parent's horrible, nasty divorce. I did not know how to handle the pain and so I ate, stuffing down the emotions and the confusion. I remember my brother and his anger, punching me day after day calling me "fatty, fat pig," every chance he got – literally beating it into my psyche.

I hear my mother's voice, "It would be a dream come true if you would only get thin," and her boyfriend John, "If she were my daughter, I would kick her ass until she lost weight," and the blind date who told me, "You would be incredible if you were only svelte." I took it all in, believing I was flawed and not worthy of love unless I am thin.

I cry in the bathroom until there are no more tears and return to the table. What else can I do? I am in the middle of nowhere with strangers. I suppose I could take a cab to Sarria, but something inside of me says, *No keep walking*.

Back at the table, I am quiet. Raphael knows he has hurt me. Somehow feeling the need to defend myself, I say, "This is my body, my size, what can I do?" He proceeds to tell me how much weight he has lost since starting the Camino.

At this point, I want to punch him in the face and scream, "You have no right to say anything about anybody's body unless you are asked for your opinion. You know nothing about me, how dare you! On this walk, I have not even been thinking about "the weight," so f__k you very much for reminding me!"

After this, I just want to walk alone and isolate myself, which is my habit, and process what just happened. But I keep walking without speaking, because if I say anything I might really start crying and I don't want the others to see me cry. I don't want them to see the pain Raphael has caused me.

He speaks first, "If I said something to hurt you, I am very sorry. I have disturbed your Camino and understand if you would like to walk alone."

"It's cruel to call someone heavy," I say. I don't understand why I feel a need to explain my body to him. I just want him to know how deeply he has hurt me.

He apologizes again, saying he is ashamed and did not mean to insult me. This does not help or make me feel better. I can tell he is sincere, sad and now he is tearing up. He says something about how Americans are crazy about all this body image stuff. *Yep, that's right.* How could he have known this is my biggest issue, quite frankly, the one that has held me back from so much for so many years. I have taken in the negative words and criticisms from others and believed it to be true. Oh, how I have prayed and begged God to take it all away and to please help me in learning to love and accept myself. Trying to forgive, and knowing from a metaphysical/spiritual point of view that I created it all, they were all just reflections of how I felt about myself.

Now here I am on the Camino feeling good about myself, and I'm wondering how one stupid ass comment could affect me so much and bring me to despair.

Raphael apologizes again, "I am so sorry to have disturbed your Camino, and I understand if you would like to walk alone." I don't know why, but I stay with him. Perhaps this experience will prove to be a valuable healing, a deep letting go of long-held illusions and emotions.

We are quiet. I am walking powerfully, channeling this energy into the walk, making it up steep hills strong and fast, as if to say, "Look! Look at what this heavy body can do!"

We walk on chatting a bit, but mostly we are quiet, listening to the sounds of nature. Hearing the birds, the breeze, and far off cowbells, I feel "it" is still there. I feel the sadness and embarrassment of never being able to get a handle on "the weight." How it is out there on display for everyone to see and criticize, and I realize it has always just been my own intense criticism of myself.

The clouds and shade are gone now and the path turns to asphalt under the blazing sun, which hurts my feet even more. It seems to go on forever – how much further will we walk. There is nothing in sight, except more road.

A young guy comes up behind us, walking slowly. Joseph is twenty-two years old and from Ireland. He is tall and thin, and he tells us his feet and back are hurting badly. I want to say to Raphael, "Look, a young, thin guy and his f__king feet hurt, too" I didn't say anything, but I believe Raphael understood.

Now all of us are hurting and wondering where in the hell the next town is. After several more miles, we finally see a small town with a bar/café and we all cheer. Already seated at a table in the shade are the two girls from earlier and Raphael's German friends. I'm going to order an Aquarius. I see Raphael has ordered a beer, the kind with lemonade I've been hearing about. I look at it thirstily, sitting on the bar in an ice-cold mug. Raphael hands it to me. Is this his peace offering? I accept it gladly and find it delicious as it quenches my thirst. We all order insalata mista, take off our shoes, clink glasses, and cheers in four different languages.

Three miles to go. I change into my sandals, pop an ibuprofen, and walk on with Raphael. I am walking slowly now with a slight limp; the sun is high and hot. Raphael stays with me to the beginning of the town where his hostel is located. We say our goodbyes, hug, and double cheek kiss. I'm relieved to move on by myself. It's been quite a day.

My three-star hotel has air-conditioning. Hooray for that! I shower and rest with my legs up the wall, and then venture out to find a market, already knowing I will stay in tonight. As I sit in my room contemplating the events of the day, the tears come again, expressing the hurt I have held inside for so long. I let them come: the pain and the feelings, the ones that need healing. The tears come strongly releasing my pain. *Dear God, please get this out of me.* Finally, I sleep deeply and peacefully.

Day Thirty-One

"What the universe will manifest when you are in alignment
with it is a lot more interesting than what you try to manifest."

—Adyashanti

I LEAVE EARLY, BEFORE BREAKFAST, AND WALK THROUGH
the town as the sun is rising. It's all up hill and already I
can feel the strain in my feet and legs. I stop at a bar for
breakfast and a short rest, and continue on. When I stop
to snap a few photos of the sunrise and the lovely view over
the town, I see a young couple also taking photos. As they
get near, I can tell they are American. We greet each other
and they ask if I just started walking. "No," I tell them. I
started from St. Jean."

They look surprised and ask why they haven't seen me
before. I don't know – another mystery of the Camino.
They're in their early twenties and on a break from college.
He has just finished a semester in Nepal, so I ask if he was
there during the recent devastating earthquake. Yes, actually they both were. She had arrived two days before the
quake to meet up with him. They were on a crowded bus
when it hit. They could see the road ahead of them rippling

like asphalt waves. They did not know what it was. People on the bus were screaming, crying, and praying. They had a small amount of water and some protein bars with them because they were heading out for a hike. After the quake, it took several days to make it back to Kathmandu and his host family. Thankfully, they were all safe. He said all he wanted to do was stay and help, but he realized this was his ego speaking. If he stayed, he would be taking their limited food and water, so he decided it was best was for him to leave and return at a later date.

They made their way to India, where they just happened on a teaching by the Dalai Lama. Then they traveled around, and now they are here on the Camino. They are quite a lovely, well-traveled, open-minded couple. We walk and talk together for several hours, and I'm thinking that if all young people could travel and live abroad for a while, the world would be a better place. I thoroughly enjoy my time with them, until they move on and I stop for a much-needed rest and refreshing break.

Continuing on my own, at this stage the Camino is getting crowded with many people who are walking only the last hundred kilometers. When they reach Santiago, they will be eligible for the Compostela, or Certificate.

Once again, I feel somewhat invaded because of the huge groups and all the loud (very loud) talking. I keep to myself, continuing to forgive all, especially myself. The heat is suffocating. This is the hottest day on the Camino, so far. At least I am somewhat used to it living in the desert of Southern California. I notice some pilgrims from Ireland and the U.K. with very red faces. I feel for them when they tell me they have never experienced this kind of heat. I take several more breaks for water and Aquarius, and finally make it to Portomarin, a large town on a lake. There seems to be some boating and kayaking available, but surprisingly there is no one out on the water. I stop and ask directions, and make it up another hill to my hotel. It's pleasant, but there is no air conditioning on this, the hottest day. What a big bummer! It seems I am on a continuous hot-flash!

I go for another late lunch meal and spend the rest of the evening resting and reading before going to bed early.

Day Thirty-Two

*"The pure perfect truth of life is that we are here to create
heaven on earth, to bring the perfection of what is above down
to us, and in doing so to become transformed as human being
into something great and beautiful."*

—Kathleen McGowan, from *The Poet Prince*

WAKING UP THIS MORNING, I'M FEELING TIRED AND GROGGY.
The room was nice but stifling hot. The open window pro-
vided a light breeze but also the sounds of late night partiers.

After a protein-filled breakfast of eggs, ham, cheese,
toast, orange, juice and coffee, I hit the road. I'm not looking forward to the crowds today, but it does look like it
will be cooler. For this I am grateful. Leaving town, I see
there are many pilgrims starting out as well. As I walk, the
crowd thins out and the way moves into rural farmland. My
thoughts return to my past and my family. I contemplate my
parents and think of how they met and married, so young,
attractive, and in love. I contemplate change, the constant
change in all of our lives – my parent's horrible divorce, my
sadness, and the beginning of filling myself with food and
sugar to try and make the pain go away.

I walk on thinking about my teenage years and my twenties – school, friends, boyfriends, my start in the restaurant business, the places I lived, and way too much partying – my thirties, forties, and now my fifties. I think about my move back to Palm Desert in 2000 and the start of my catering business, how it grew at the perfect pace. My dream of a gourmet market and wine shop materialized in 2006 after a devastating restaurant partnership experience ended. (Another story for another time.)

As I walk the Camino, I see so many different people, all with their own unique story. I realize deep down that we all want the same basic things. To live a good life, to be happy, have security, and most of all to have love.

I contemplate and I am grateful for all the circumstances of my life that have gotten me right here, right now on the Camino. I am grateful for the many lessons learned over the years that have made me a more compassionate human being. I am grateful also for every relationship, especially the "bad" tough ones that have taught me more about love and respect for myself and others.

I make it to Palas De Rei as the rain starts. The hotel is a complex that looks like a huge wooden cabin. Lush green grass and pine and chestnut trees surround it. The lobby and restaurant are lively and filled with demanding pilgrims. I have a quick late lunch in the bar and spend the evening in my room. I open the windows and listen to the pouring rain and once again the tears come as I pray. "Please, I want to live fully and happily. Let me shine in the world. Let me help and be of service. I must love myself; this old stuff, these old beliefs must go!

Please, please, please, Amen

"I have an everyday religion that works for me. Love yourself first and everything else falls into line."

—Lucille Ball

Day Thirty-Three

*"Dear God, Show me the truth about myself,
no matter how beautiful it is."*

—Anonymous

*"Don't be quick to interpret the moment. Just keep quiet.
My encouragement would always be: never think anything
is against you, everything is a blessing. Why should it be
different? Just be quiet. Let it all work itself out."*

—Mooji

I SLEEP WELL AND WAKE AT 5:00 A.M. READY TO GET ON
the road at 6:00. There are just three more days of walking,
and I am so ready to get to Santiago. I must focus on love
today, love of myself, love for all, no judgment, and no pain
or suffering.

The morning starts out misty and cool with shaded
wooded paths. It is quiet for a while, but before long the
pilgrims are everywhere, talking, talking, talking. After so
much silence, it sounds like they are yelling. This is not a
judgment, but rather a simple statement that the noise is
hard to bear. Walking is difficult today and one coffee on an

empty stomach does not help! I feel quite lethargic. About an hour in, I stop for water and a tortilla.

The food perks me up, but I'm in no hurry. I walk, grateful for the cooler weather today, but I feel like I am totally done. I just do not want to do this anymore, but I am in the middle of nowhere so there is not much of a choice. Then I remember: *Turn it over to the Divine*

I feel like I could collapse, just lie down and die. This might sound overly dramatic but, seriously, this is how I feel, and so I pray.

My Prayer

Please, God, take over. Walk through me. Walk in me.
I let go. I am light. I am free. I forgive.
I really do want to live. I want to laugh. I want to love.
I surrender to Your will. Align my will with Yours and take over.

It works. I keep walking and praying, walking and praying. I come to a café and order water and a muffin. This helps, and I am able to keep moving. If I can make it to the town of Melide, which still makes it a 10-mile day, I will be done and cab it.

I come to a town that is likely to be Melide. I go into the church, get my stamp, snap a photo, and notice a side street with a quiet bar. There are two girls in the bar ordering beer. The beer looks really good, cold and frosty, so I order one too. The girls are from Norway, and they invite me to sit with them. They say, "We just started walking today. How about you?"

When I tell them I've been walking for thirty-three days, their jaws drop and eyes widen in surprise. We talk about their travels and the Camino. They are twenty-eight and delightful. I am grateful for this short break with them. After finishing our beers, we walk together for a while, wish each other "Buen Camino," and say we hope to see each other again.

I walk another half mile into town, find a pizzeria, and order a glass of Albarino (the delicious white wine of the region) and a pizza margarita. As I enjoy my meal, a couple with a young child comes and sits behind me. They are walking the Camino with a toddler in a stroller! Unbelievable! The child is screaming and crying. The weary parents are saying, "Stop, stop," but the screaming escalates. Usually this would really bother me, but for some reason I am fine with it. I send love and light to the child and parents, and eventually the child becomes quiet. I finish eating and am ready for my cab.

The cabdriver keeps pointing out the Camino, as if I cannot see the pilgrims walking. It seems like a long ride, which means it would have been a very long walk. I have no guilt and am happy I chose the cab.

The hotel is okay, even though I'm given a noisy room on the street. When a truck drives by, it feels like an earthquake in the room. It seems I am getting used to anything. I wash a few things (along with myself) in the shower and hang them out the window to dry. I feel so tired, physically and emotionally.

Dinner is at 7:30. This restaurant has gotten very good reviews on Trip Advisor and the food is good. But it's just more of the same: salad, roast chicken, potatoes, house wine, and Santiago cake for dessert – which I take to my room and devour, not that I am still hungry, mind you. I must make a note that the staff here at the hotel and restaurant are excellent.

With two more days to walk, I'm ready for this experience to be over.

Day Thirty-Four

"Healing is available to you now, unless you believe the will of God takes time.... Every decision you make indicates what you believe you are worth."

—*A Course in Miracles*

I woke up a few times during the night because the walls are thin and I could hear the guys snoring in the next room, which means they could probably hear me snoring, as well! Even after sleeping, I feel drained and have no motivation to continue. After all this effort, I can't help but wonder, *what has this all been for?* Frankly, the physical part has been very difficult and probably not the healthiest – time will tell as to the emotional and spiritual part. Right now, I am too depleted to try and comprehend how I might feel when I return home.

Starting at 6:30 a.m., as the sun is just starting to come up, I walk out of the city on uneven cobblestone streets. Already my feet are not happy. I will go as far as I can and get another cab, if need be. The cobblestone stops at the end of the city and turns into a dirt path lined with trees. Some I recognize as Aspen and eucalyptus. They are majestic and peaceful and seem to be welcoming me. There are groups of pilgrims passing by, but mostly I am alone. Strange, I think as there are so many walking and still I am alone.

I walk until eight o'clock and stop at the first café for coffee and toast. There are many pilgrims here, and I overhear one group making arrangements for beds in Santiago tonight! TONIGHT! That would mean about 25 miles for them. I cannot even fathom it.

Continuing on, the path is shady and cool. I'm beginning to see more people on the road: singles, couples, and groups; some are quiet and many talking loudly. I try not to criticize or judge, recognizing this is their Camino, too. My feet are hurting and my legs cannot move very fast, at this point. Many other pilgrims are quickly walking past me. *How are they walking so fast?* I wonder.

Once again handing it over to the Divine, I pray: *I am done. If You want me to continue, please take over.*

My breathing is shallow and it's hard to take a deep satisfying breath. I stop to rest and drink another glass of sparkling water and Aquarius. I keep going, walking as fast as I can, which is not very fast. The surrounding scenery is beautiful, wild daisies and gorgeous hydrangeas in white, pink, blue, and purple. I try to breathe it all in, but I want to move faster.

The anger boils up inside me again, and I speak out loud, in a loud whisper, "Is anybody there? Does anyone hear me? I need help. I keep asking and asking and offering myself. Is this all a big f__king joke? A lie? Why is no one helping me? How much must I ask and pray?"

I am pissed off, frustrated and depressed, and I get why people want to hurt themselves, check out, even commit suicide. I absolutely get it! Why is it so hard to just be happy?

I understand feeling worthless, like a complete failure and just tired of all this. I GET IT!

Finally, the tears come, angry pissed off tears, and still I continue walking.

Arriving at a cafe, no one acknowledges me when I walk in. There are only a few people sitting at the bar. The waitress looks at me and says nothing. This really makes me mad, and I say loudly with a fake smile, "HOLA!" She hesitates and then returns my "Hola."

I ask for food and get the alien look. She hands me a menu, as if I am interrupting her. I order a beer and she looks at me blankly. Isn't the word "beer" kind of universal? I point to the keg handle...beer! She asks, "One?"

I feel like screaming, "No I want ten. Yes, one f___king beer. Have you ever heard of customer service?" But, of course, I say nothing.

Sitting outside, I wait for a tuna sandwich, watching as she waits on another table of locals. She brings them wine and tapas. She is friendly and laughing with them. I drink my beer and I'm ready to get up and leave when she finally brings out my sandwich. It is a terrible sandwich. I am sick of tuna and bread. I eat a fourth of it, pay, and move on.

Now that I am feeling my deep down anger, I forget the pain in my feet, the beer and an ibuprofen help. I keep walking, figuring I can get a cab when I get to the next town. The path is easy and the anger subsides a bit. I can't help but notice how pleasant my surroundings are, but I am stubborn and want to stay angry and hang on to the crappy feelings. I'm determined not to enjoy anything.

I get to the turn-off for the town and it's filled with pilgrims having a good time. I keep walking. *Walk it off* I tell myself. *Walk it off; walk it off.*

I come to a path I imagine to be like the Sherwood

Forest, shady, quiet, and haunting. There is no one in front of me and no one behind me, but I am not afraid. In fact, I dare anyone to mess with me at this point. I don't know where I am, or how far I might have to go, but there are markers along the path, so I know I'm going in the right direction.

Now, I must admit, it is beautiful. I take out my phone and snap some photos. My mind has quieted down, now that the anger is spent, and I simply walk. I try looking at the map, but it doesn't tell me where I am or how long I have been walking. It seems like it should be one to four kilometers, but I don't know for sure.

I make it to the hotel, take a bath, and go down for a late lunch. The staff here is quite welcoming. The restaurant is more elegant than usual and has great service. After a lunch of fresh fish, salad, and wine, I head back upstairs to my peaceful room. I lie down and put on some of my favorite yoga music. The tears come again and I welcome them. I sob and sob and sob. Thinking about the events of the day, the entire Camino, and the support from home, I cry until there are no tears left and I am exhausted. I lay down my yoga mat and stretch, and put my legs up the wall – while listening to the beautiful voice of Deva Premal. Finally, for the first time today, I feel at peace. I stay in my room for the evening and go to bed at 8:30, after reading all the support from my friends on Facebook. It is quite humbling and heartwarming and I feel blessed.

Day Thirty-Five

*"When emotions come, as they inevitably will,
dance them, move them, and confront people, situations,
and challenges from a point of centered stillness.
Blocked emotions end up exploding or festering and have
much more impact than they should."*

—Gabrielle Roth

I SLEEP WELL, WAKING A FEW TIMES TO NOISE IN THE HALL-way. I plan on leaving by seven. Only 10 miles today and I'm hoping to make it to Santiago by 11:30, but who knows. I've realized that I cannot make plans on the Camino.

The morning starts out quite misty; the air is cool and feels good on my skin. I walk past a small airport and the sounds of the planes are deafening, bringing me back to reality. I chat and walk for a while with a family from Colorado; these parents and their six kids are walking the Camino together, I thoroughly enjoy their company. They stop to eat and I walk on alone. I feel very emotional as I get closer to Santiago, I want to be done, but then what?

I make it to the outskirts of the city and get a photo taken in front of the Camino de Santiago sign. Continuing into the city, I turn a corner and see the top spires of the Cathedral. I run into a couple of women I met a few days before. We hug and offer each other congratulations – we are all very emotional. I keep moving through the narrow streets, which are crowded with people, restaurants, bars, and souvenir shops filled with Camino memorabilia.

As I enter the Cathedral Plaza, I am a bit numb. I still can't quite believe I am finally here – after thirty-five days. Many people are milling around, celebrating, taking photos, kneeling and kissing the ground. I find my hotel, another gorgeous restored monastery which is right across the street from the cathedral, drop my pack, and head on over.

It is 11:00 a.m. and the Pilgrims' Mass starts at noon. I am not religious in the usual sense of the word, nor Catholic, but I do believe in Jesus and his true teachings. Most incredible of all is that the cathedral contains the Tomb of the Apostle James the Greater. Pilgrims have been coming to Santiago since its early beginnings in 829 AD. The building is a Romanesque structure, with later Gothic and Baroque additions. The results of all the building and rebuilding are truly breathtaking.

Traditionally, pilgrims touch the pillar just inside the doorway of the cathedral when entering. So many of them have touched it over the centuries that the stone has been worn away. Inside, many pilgrims have gathered for Mass; the excitement and devotion can be felt by all.

I walk around, taking photos of the visual feast of gold, glitter, stone, and statuary. The church is filling up and the large crowd is overwhelming, so I say a prayer and leave. Not being Catholic, I don't understand the meaning of the Mass, anyway.

Heading up the street to a bar for something to eat, I see Jay from North Carolina. I have not seen him for weeks and thought he was long gone. Jay arrived in Santiago three days before me. We talk about our experiences and he walks me over to the Compostela office to get my certificate. The Pilgrim's Office gives out more than 100,000 certificates every year to pilgrims from more than 100 different countries. Here is what it says on my certificate:

"The Holy Apostolic Metropolitan Cathedral of Santiago de Compostela expresses its warm welcome to the Tomb of the Apostle St. James the Greater; and wishes that the holy Apostle may grant you, in abundance, the graces of the Pilgrimage."

HEADING BACK TO THE HOTEL, I FEEL DRAINED AND depressed. I'm wondering what my "graces" will be in the coming months, or years. It all seems anticlimactic. I did it. I'm done. This is what I wanted, so why am I feeling depressed?

Trying to rest in my room, I am antsy, yet not sure what to do. I'm not in the mood to write. I attempt to contemplate what I have just accomplished in completing the Camino, and what might be next, but nothing comes. I have been emptied out.

I meet up with Jay again around seven. We have a few drinks on our own and arrange to have dinner with some of his friends later. I tell him how I feel, and he says he feels it, too – and so do most of the friends he finished with. We are all glad to be done, but also feel the emotional and physical drain and sadness at saying goodbye.

Jay tells me about a woman he met from Norway – now remember, Jay was walking to help his healing from a second divorce. But then he meets this woman in the last week and believes he has found "Camino love." This is it. She's the "one." They make future plans to be together, but she ends it abruptly with no explanation and leaves. Jay feels like he just went through another divorce and he is sad and confused.

I believe the Camino definitely works on you, your issues, and your karma. It's like you work through lifetimes of accumulated "stuff" while walking for days on this ancient sacred path.

We walk around town for an hour trying to find the restaurant, and when we do the group welcomes us: ten Portuguese and two American women. I wish I had met them sooner, because I really like them. The restaurant is very noisy, making it hard to communicate. Everything is so overwhelming. There is lots of wine and the food is ordered family style; there are seafood specialties, octopus, mussels, and shrimp cooked several different ways, no veggies or salad in sight. After dinner, we head out together and walk around town for a while. It's a lovely evening, filled with people, street performers, and celebrating pilgrims. It's just starting to get dark at 10:30 p.m., and when I stop to listen to a musician realize I have lost the group.

When I get back to my room, there is a text from Jay asking if I am okay. They were all concerned that they had lost me, very sweet. "Yes, I am fine," I text back. "Thanks for a fun evening and nice to meet everyone." We make a plan to share a cab to the airport the next day.

The next morning I wake up early and head down to breakfast. The café is noisy and crowded, and I eat quickly. I'm feeling melancholy and tired, and just don't know what to think or do about anything. The only thing I know is to walk. I like the mornings in the cities in Spain, they are cool and quiet. I walk all around Santiago, and to the outskirts.

I must say, it feels good to walk. I don't know where I am and don't care. I keep walking for an hour and a half. I find a quiet park that is deserted. I sit in the shade of a large tree and close my eyes. Feeling my heart and mind open, I receive a very clear message, "It is time to take your power back."

The Camino markers lead me back to the cathedral, and by the time I get back to my hotel, I'm feeling much better.

On the front steps up walks Raphael, who I had not seen since "that" day. We hug and exchange some Camino stories. It is good to see him, all has been forgiven. He and his friend invite me to hang out with them, but I tell him, "No thanks. I'm going to Madrid and then home." We say our goodbyes and a final "Buen Camino."

I pack up, get a cab, pick up Jay, and we leave together for the Santiago airport. We talk about the Camino, our experiences, and how we will really not be able to adequately describe the Camino, what happens on the Camino, the magic and the pain of the Camino, and especially the love on the Camino. Walking the Camino is like living a whole lifetime in thirty-five days. I feel much of my karma has been worked through and I am filled with gratitude.

Thank you Camino

After The Camino

"Holy are you, eternal, free and whole, at peace forever in the Heart of God."
"You are the work of God, and his work is wholly lovable and wholly loving. This is how a man must think of himself in his heart, because this is what he is."

—*A Course in Miracles*

FINISHING THE CAMINO IS BITTERSWEET. I FEEL JOYFUL AT having finished, but I am left with many unanswered questions. I suppose what I really wanted was to be done with working on my "stuff," and to come out of the experience fully enlightened! But what I found myself thinking was, *I am still me, so what's next?*

It has been said that your Camino starts once you make a plan to walk it, and also that it does not start until after you have finished walking it. I was very happy to be going home and filled with hope about my unknown future.

The rest of summer 2015 passed quickly. My mind was already reeling with planning another Camino. As much as I wanted to finish the first one, now I really missed it and wanted to go back! The Camino definitely had a profound effect on me. I am proud of myself for embarking on such a journey alone and completing it. As I was contemplating a second Camino, my friend Meredith, who had been following me on Facebook, suggested I take a group with me. At first, I rolled my eyes and said, "Yes, maybe someday." In truth, I would not even know how to begin.

I must thank her, however, because she kept pushing me. She suggested I simply put it out there and see what the response might be. I researched different routes and decided on the Portuguese coastal route, setting the date for June 2016. We would meet in Porto, Portugal for a twelve-night, eleven-day pilgrimage to Santiago. I consulted guidebooks and researched the towns, hotels, and luggage transport. I put a very reasonable price tag on it, enough to cover my costs plus a little extra for my time.

Several women signed up immediately. Most of them said the Camino had been on their bucket list for a long time, but they did not want to do it alone. The group dynamic appealed to them.

As I worked and cooked my way through my 2016 season, I also planned the next journey, this time with a group. The final count was fifteen, including me. There were fourteen women and one man – he was the husband of one of the women. They had not taken a vacation in many years.

The people in the group ranged in age from 45 to 75. We met in Porto, filled with enthusiasm and ready to embark on an adventure. Lifelong friendships were formed and the camaraderie of the group was heartwarming. Once again, I was immersed in Camino magic! Every pilgrim in our group finished with wide-open hearts and joyful smiles. We were left with many fond memories and ready for new beginnings. Everyone agreed it was one of the best trips ever, and many vowed to return for another Camino.

As for me, I have found a new purpose and passion

through introducing and guiding people on this magical, mystical path. Now I am planning to escalate my efforts and create group journeys to other sacred places around the world. I am looking forward to many more group trips.

I realize walking the Camino gave me the opportunity to completely focus on myself. I encouraged and allowed all the old junky stuff to surface – basically, anything inside me that was not love. I let go of everything I possibly could that was keeping me from being fully free, alive, and living the life of my dreams. I released all of the anger, sadness, self-loathing, and judgment that I was able to release, letting it be transformed into love and compassion for others and myself.

A Course in Miracles says we cannot get to Heaven alone. We must include everyone, EVERYONE! We must help and serve others along the way. We are all connected and in this together – especially the people we disagree with or do not like, and the ones who commit unimaginable hateful acts. These are the ones who need the most healing and the most love.

We must put our egos aside, step back, and let Divine Love flow through us, always. Can you imagine what this world would be like? We are so powerful – our thoughts are so powerful.

If there is something we judge or do not like about someone, we must bring it back to ourselves, because everyone we encounter is a perfect reflection of us. This also goes for beauty, love, and peace. When we see this, we see our perfection.

I do not know what my future holds, and it does not really matter, because most of the time I feel at peace, blessed, and grateful for this journey.

RECOMMENDED READING

Laws of Life: The Teachings of Yogi Bhajan by Yogi Bhajan and Kaur Khalsa;

Kundalini Research Institute: Santa Cruz, NM; 2013.

The Tao Te Ching: A New English Version by Lao Tzu and Stephen Mitchell; Harper Perennial Modern Classics: New York, New York; 2006.

A Course in Weight Loss: 21 Spiritual Lessons for Surrendering Your Weight Forever by Marianne Williamson; Hay House: Carlsbad, CA; 2012.

The Grass Grows By Itself: Bhagwan Shree Rajneesh Talks on Zen by Bhagwan Shree Rajneesh; The Rajneesh Foundation; 1978.

A Course in Miracles, Foundation for Inner Peace, by the scribe: Dr. Helen Schucman; Foundation for Inner Peace: Temecula, CA; 1975.

I Know Why the Caged Bird Sings by Maya Angelou with Forward by Oprah Winfrey; Random House: New York, N.Y.; 2009.

Who Am I? The Teaching of Bhagavan Sri Ramana Maharishi by Sri Ramana Maharishi; Sri Ramana Ashram; 2007.

Letting Go, The Pathway of Surrender by David R. Hawkins; Hay House: Carlsbad, California; 2014.

Sadhana of the Heart: A Collection of Talks on Spiritual Life by Gurumayi Chidvilasananda; Siddha Yoga Publications: 2007.

The Alchemist by Paulo Coelho; HarperTorch; 1988

Blood Memory: An Autobiography by Martha Graham; Doubleday: New York, New York; 1991.

The Gift: Poems by the Great Sufi Master by Hafiz and Daniel Ladinsky; Penguin Compass: New York, New York; 1999.

The Four Agreements: A Practical Guide to Personal Freedom (A Toltec Wisdom Book by Don Miguel Ruiz and Janet Mills; Amber-Allan Publishing: San Rafael, California; 1997.

Out of My Life and Thought: An Autobiography by Albert Schweitzer and Antje B. Lemke; John Hopkins University Press: Baltimore, Maryland; 2009.

The Essential Rumi, New Expanded Edition by Jalal al-din Rumi and Coleman Banks; HarperOne: New York; 2004.

Gandhi: An Autobiography – The Story of My Experiments with Truth by Mohandas K. "Mahatma" Gandhi; Beacon Press: Manchester, United Kingdom; 1993.

Walden: Life in the Woods by Henry David Thoreau; CreateSpace Publications Platform; 2017.

The Color Purple by Alice Walker; Mariner Books/Houghton Miffin/Harcourt: Boston, Massachusetts; 2003.

The Science of Mind: Complete Edition by Ernest Holmes; Tarcher-Perigee/Penguin: New York, New York; 2010.

Living on Love: The Messenger by Klaus Joehle; iUniverse; 2001.

Entering the Castle: Finding the Inner Path to God and Your Soul's Purpose by Caroline Myss; Atria Books: New York, New York; 2008.

Seriously, I'm Kidding by Ellen DeGeneres; Grand Central Publishing/Hachette: New York, New York; 2012.

The Diary of Anais Nin by Anais Nin; Mariner Books/ Houghton/Miffin/Harcourt: Boston, Massachusetts; 1969.

Return to Joy by Andrew Harvey and W. Carolyn Baker; iUniverse; 2016.

The Law of Attraction: The Basic Teachings of Abraham by Esther Abraham and Jerry Hicks; Hay House: Carlsbad, California; 2006.

Johnathan Livingston Seagull: The Complete Edition by Richard Bach; Scribner: New York, New York; 2014.

The Teachings of Don Juan: A Yaqui Way of Knowledge by Carlos Castaneda; Washington Square Press/Simon & Schuster; New York, New York; 1985.

Gorgeous for God: Awakening through a Course in Miracles by Lisa Natoli; Author House; 2013

Miracles by Stuart Wilde; Hay House: Carlsbad, California; 2008.

The Way of Liberation: A Practical Guide to Spiritual Enlightenment by Adyashanti; Open Gate Sanga; San Francisco, California; 2013.

The Expected One, The Book of Love and The Poet Price by Kathleen McGowan; Simon and Schuster

Vaster Than Sky, Greater Than Space: What You Are Before You Became by Mooji; Sounds True: Louisville, Colorado; 2016.

Maps to Ecstacy: The Healing Power of Movement by Gabrielle Roth; New World Library: San Francisco: California; 1998.

Be Here Now by Ram Dass; Lama Foundation: Taos, New Mexico; 1978.

You Can Heal Your Life by Louise Hay; Hay House: Carlsbad, California; 1984.

Many Lives, Many Masters: The True Story of a Prominent Psychiatrist, His Young Patient, and the Past-Life Therapy That Changed Both Their Lives by Brian Weiss; Fireside Publishing; 1988.

Out on a Limb by Shirley MacLaine; Bantam Books: New York, New York; 1986.

I Am an Emotional Creature: The Secret Life of Girls Around the World by Eve Ensler; Villard/Random House: New York, New York. 2011.

ABOUT THE AUTHOR

Since her solo journey on the Camino de Santiago in 2015, Jennifer Winn Johnson has spent her summers introducing fellow travelers to the Camino. These group tours, which she offers through her travel company, Winn Journeys, offer a different and expanded view of this sacred path. During the winter season, Jennifer is a caterer in Rancho Mirage, California, where she lives with her two rescue dogs.

More information at
www.WinnJourneys.com

or contact *winnjourneys@gmail.com*

Made in the USA
Columbia, SC
30 March 2018